Advance praise for Mind Alchemy

Cayce is a transformational leader and her experience will benefit your journey of personal and professional growth. She is a modern mystic who has helped thousands, you can trust her to guide you into practical experiences of connection with God.

- Tracy Goss, World's leading authority on Executive Reinvention, lecturer and author of *The Last Word on Power*

One of my earliest memories is entering into a relationship with Jesus. Since then, I have been able to sit at the feet of (learn from) some of the leading teachers of our generation. However, Cayce is the only one who finally, when I desperately needed guidance from the Father, showed me practically how to achieve what is most important in this "relationship" we call Christianity—intimacy with the Creator of the universe. Her book and the One Journey will open up, for those who are ready, a world that most Christians never get to experience.

- Jonathan Chen, Business strategist, leadership consultant and student of the One Journey

I have had the joy of knowing Cayce for over 25 years. She has a gift of invitation and permission. An invitation to discover who you really are and permission to actually live in the fullness of it. Her loving, nonjudgmental presence provides a space of possibility and clarity. That is what she has co-created with her team at One and that is what you will find in *Mind Alchemy*. Invitation, permission, possibility and clarity to actually live in the freedom and joy of who you are created to be.

- Anne Marie Bailey, Singer-songwriter

Cayce's experience and wisdom have helped me grow in my ability to move past limited thinking and into all that God has for me, my family, our business and our community. A must read for practical growth and life-changing practices.

- Scott Barr, Owner/steward Southwest Exteriors

Cayce Harris' style and substance really cannot be matched. Her thoughts, both visionary and lofty, always come with practical how to's and have helped me and many others time and again. I have no doubt that this book will bear much fruit for those seeking a transformed mind.

- Rosalind Hervey, Spiritual mentor and co-creator/co-leader of the One Journey

MIND ALCHEMY

*7 Practices to Transform
What Threatens You into Gold*

CAYCE YATES HARRIS

MIND ALCHEMY

7 Practices to Transform What Threatens You into Gold

© 2023, Cayce Yates Harris.

Print ISBN: 979-8-35092-811-2

eBook ISBN: 979-8-35092-812-9

For my mom.
She's humble, brilliant, and
as some have said, an actual angel.

Contents

SECTION ONE— INTRODUCTION TO MIND ALCHEMY

From Oxford Languages Online

MIND

noun

1. the element of a person that enables them to be aware of the world and their experiences, to think, and to feel; the faculty of **consciousness** and thought.
    "as the thoughts ran through his mind, he came to a conclusion"

2. a person's **intellect**.
    "his keen mind"
    > a person's memory.
    > *"the company's name **slips my mind**"*

3. a person's **attention**.
    "I expect my employees to keep their minds on the job"
    > the will or determination to achieve something.
    > *"anyone can lose weight if they set their mind to it"*

verb

1. be **distressed, annoyed, or worried** by.
    "I don't mind the rain"
    > have an objection to.
    > *"what does that mean, if you don't mind my asking?"*

2. be **reluctant** to do something (often used in polite requests).
    "*I don't mind admitting I was worried*"

    INFORMAL

    used to express one's strong **enthusiasm** for something.
    "*I wouldn't mind some coaching from him!*"

3. **regard** as important; **feel concern about.**
    "*never mind the opinion polls*"

4. be **inclined** or **disposed** to do a particular thing.
    "*he was minded to reject the application*"

Origin

Old English gemynd "memory, thought," of Germanic origin, from an Indo-European root meaning 'revolve in the mind, think,' shared by Sanskrit manas and Latin mens "mind."

AL·CHE·MY

/ˈalkəmē/

noun

noun: **alchemy**

the medieval **forerunner** of chemistry, based on the supposed transformation of matter. It was concerned particularly with attempts to **convert base metals into gold** or to find a universal **elixir.**

a seemingly magical process of transformation, creation, or combination.
"*finding the person who's right for you requires a very subtle alchemy*"

Origin

Late Middle English: via Old French and medieval Latin from Arabic *al-kīmiyā*', from *al* "the" + *kīmiyā*' (from Greek *khēmia, khēmeia* 'art of transmuting metals').

Try this book.

There's a journey we share regardless of where we come from and where we're going. It's the human journey. What is it to be human? What experiences are universally human? What actually inspires us and what deeply threatens us?

Mind Alchemy is for people ready to dismantle threats as they come across the screen of our minds.

This book will help anyone who wants to experience the connection that already exists between your own thoughts, God's thoughts, and the voices of the world around you.

This book is not for people who "believe" certain things about their minds and God's mind. It's for anyone who wants to explore the genuine connection that is built in. Not only is the connection built-in but so is the invitation. It's innate in every single human life—the invitation to connection and experiential interconnectedness is extended, processed, engaged, and enjoyed through what you and I call our "minds."

Our minds already process in a way that's conducive to experiencing oneness (connection, union) with God. What is oneness? How is it practical for everyday life? What do your regular thoughts have to do with it? Not only will you know by the end of the book, you'll know through experience and that is an entirely different kind of knowledge. That's what alchemy is all about—taking something basic and turning it into something far more valuable, like turning common metal into gold. You can turn your seemingly everyday thoughts into a productive, helpful, and integrated part of a much greater whole. You were made to easily navigate a flow state of mind, bringing health to your own life and connection to the greater flow of life that surrounds you. Somewhere along the way we lost a practical application for the how-to of the very intuitive flow that we were created for.

Reading *Mind Alchemy* will be an experience, and it will help you develop a practice that you can use long after you've put the book down. I wrote this book for you to experiment with. Please write in the margins, use a favorite notebook, or pull up your notes app to engage the practices for yourself.

As you read you'll learn a simple process for taking any basic thought and transforming it into something far more valuable. It will still take the shape of a thought but one that can be described as far more solid. The solidity of thought comes full of the very energy you need to grow, to create, to rest, and to be truly productive and abundant throughout your lifetime.

You'll become aware of how you think. Thinking about how you think is an essential part of the process and foundational to what comes next. The next step is where the real treasure is: transform, create, and combine your thoughts in such a way that your thoughts become uniquely valuable for every aspect of your life.

Listen to *our* shared story told in the simple phrases people today most often use with the word "mind" in the mix:

Something/someone comes to mind
To close one's mind
To be open-minded
To see in one's mind's eye

To mind
To have half a mind to do something
To bear something in mind
Mind over matter
Put one's mind to
To be of one mind
On someone's mind

To be of two minds
To be of a different mind
Never mind
To give someone a piece of one's mind
Out of one's mind

The first grouping is in the realm of transformation—*awareness and unawareness.*
The second grouping is in the realm of creation—*connection and action.*
The third grouping is in the realm of combinations—*distinction and division.*

These phrases tell us that we innately know how incredibly powerful our minds are. While hinting at the powerful nature of our minds and the connection between our minds, the phrases don't fully encompass the phenomenal latent capacity and potential of our minds! Science now affirms what many have suspected about the intricacies of our minds, but what does that insight look like when it comes to the practical application for our everyday normal lives?

Our minds are capable of true alchemy.

Mind Alchemy is the practice of transforming and creating with our minds in a way that seems so easy some would describe it as magical. The process I will lead you through will happen fast, but it doesn't require what some might term "woo-woo" practices. There's no chanting, crystals, or psyche-delics required.

In actuality, it is not magical at all, it's mystical. The practice produces measurable, traceable combinations of chemical reactions within our minds, bodies, and lives. Mind alchemy changes the way we experience our lives because it starts with our thoughts and carries through to our interpretations, actions, habits, and inclinations. The mysticism you'll learn is as practical and relatable as the human body is, otherwise, it would be magical.

A pastor/teacher once told me that the real battle is in the mind. I believed him and spent years waging war. There are clear issues with this way of thinking. Here's one: to see my mind as a battlefield is to require that I am forever and always fighting myself and, by extension, others and the world. To assume that my mind is a battlefield requires that there is some eternal and internal enemy that I must detect and fight from the right side of right.

No one has the stamina to forever be at war within, just like no one has the stamina to forever be at war in the natural world. When does the soldier get to return home? When can the soldier become a farmer or artist or father or sister again? This is the question our minds will not let go of, even in the middle of the fiercest battles. Will I get home in one piece? When can I let down my guard?

What if our minds are not a war zone but at the very least, an interactive 4D map designed for navigating a grand adventure unbound by time and space?

What if our minds are not unruly and chaotic but spirited, bright, and pliable? Your mind is a spirited navigator skilled at the nearly immediate execution of a brilliant strategy. Layer into this navigation and execution system the nuances of language and emotion, and you are in a territory that is almost too wonderful for us to fathom with our minds because we are so used to living it. I won't go too far into the science because many excellent books are dedicated to this, but the element that science recently has confirmed is this: not only is your brain incredible at the way it functions in your body, it is incredible because it can function collaboratively far beyond the confines of your human skull. More on that at the end of the chapter.

Do we realize that the greatest electrical current on earth (think lightning in a bottle) is the human brain in a breathing human body? This is the reality that science now confirms.

You and your brain are lightning in a bottle, but the bottle is your incredible body that has the ability to move, bend, strengthen, feel, heal, and communicate.

Our minds will experience the occasional thunderstorm rolling through, but I promise you, that storm will water the dry and dusty soil of your world if you stop treating the raindrops like an enemy army seeking to destroy your homeland.

Like all created things, your mind is made *for you* but in its sheer power and complexity, it can seem mysterious and even antagonistic. Without training in the skills necessary to flow with the energy of your mind you may, by default, fight against it. This book will give you the tools and simple skills you can use to practice what formally has threatened your mind, and it can transform it into the gold currency you need for living freely and fully.

I'll leave you with one scientist's description of what the mind is before I tell you part of my story (emphasis in the quote below is mine).

> One aspect of the mind, beyond subjective experience, conscious-
> ness, maybe even information processing (these are facets of the
> mind that are good descriptions), let's just put those to the side
> for now, this fourth facet of the mind has a definition, not just a
> description—*this facet of the mind can be defined this way: the
> emergent self-organizing embodied and relational process that reg-
> ulates the flow of energy and information.*[1]

Mind Alchemy is an invitation from my heart to yours to step into the power-ful flow of your life that can and will only be accessed through the power of

---

1. Daniel Siegel, "A Scientific Explanation of the Human Mind," Big Think, March 5, 2017, YouTube video, 5:34, https://www.youtube.com/watch?v=C3aP905vW-c.

your mind. It's always been there for the taking from your life's first breath. Now you can know it, honor it, value it, and practice it.

What you think threatens you is actually protecting you from the greater "threat": enjoying the lifestyle of a free, empowered, and self-possessed human experience.

Life's key riddle is this: what you and I think is threatening us is not nearly as threatening as living unthreatenable.

Yes, I'm suggesting that we are all terrified of what is innate: the very being we were created to be.

We run from it very discreetly and are skilled at using shame, fear, and rejection against ourselves hoping to put distance between how we show up in the world and who we were born to be. This subconscious experience of running from, subverting, ignoring, fearing, and shaming ourselves is part of every human journey, but it is only a part, and was never meant to dominate the whole.

Here's the invitation I'm extending with the reading of this book: from this day forward, you will not settle for the lesser journey. You will take on the great adventure of upending the greatest threat you will ever face: becoming you.

I don't mean becoming who you think you need to be. I mean who you are deep down. Who you and I really, really are is what you and I are most afraid of. Why do we fear it? The why is held together by zip ties of lies. Lies we believe about ourselves, others, and God. The good news is, they are easy to cut. Mind alchemy is the process of snipping the zip ties that hold together what we think are the broken pieces of us. They are really holding together the false exterior that never really was us. When the zip ties are snipped and the packaging falls to the ground, the authentic self can emerge freely.

The seven practices you'll learn in this book will become habits that can consistently return you to joy, freedom, and belonging. This is where the real magic happens because joy, freedom, and belonging are the elements of a lifestyle of alchemy.

The fear of becoming who we are is swept under the rug by a million reasonable thoughts shaped by life experiences causing us to pile false responsibility onto our plate. Instead of reading these responsibilities as "false," we interpret them as important must-dos, proper shoulds that drown out the voice of our deeper self; the part of us that is authentic and authoritative. We give up our authority gradually, and as time passes, we normalize judging ourselves and others. As we give up our personal authority, we must assert control to counteract the loss. The cost of the exchange is a deep affirmation, and a knowing of how right we always were, are, and will be just as we are.

The magnificent human being you really are is the very thing you will consistently experience as a threat in life until that is, you understand how the threat functions and how to dismantle it.

What threatens us far more than who we are not, is who we are.

We're so threatened by it that we have told ourselves quite a story: we're not enough. We're bad. We lack. We're not important. We're selfish, prideful, and at the core, messed up. It is easy to believe this because of all the evidence we can point to but this point will never align with our origin. There is only one concept that can point to our original nature: good-natured, very good indeed.

Believing the subtle life-lie that you are lacking and not enough, stumbling through the dark and messing things up, ultimately flawed, is a linchpin story of original sin (can we let this be one of many interesting but not necessarily true narratives rather than the essentially true "Christian" narrative?). It holds you captive to what you wish was true about you but is deeply threatened by. As life happens, and we experience the fruit of incomplete thinking about self, God, others, and the world, cracks in our walls of certainty begin to appear. Cracks will form in any wall or foundation that's not built on solid ground. The foundation is a metaphor for the life that we build and what we assume about it, not for who we are.

The foundation of who you are is good soil. A solid foundation. Whatever you have built up about yourself that did not come from an understanding of your original very goodness will crack and likely, is already cracking around you. The cracks are indeed threatening, but they are the greatest gift you can receive—cracks in a house that wasn't built on a solid foundation.

What threatens you is not what you think it is. The foundation of your actual life's house is not what you think it is. It's far better.

Until we truly understand that hiding, fearing, feeling shame, rejection, and unworthiness is actually a chosen safe ground (albeit false and *unsafe*), we will never leave that territory behind.

Whatever you think you lack or need in order to become like God—more love, more patience, more study, more good choices, more theology, more time, more character— the word more is a dead giveaway that you do not know who you are or from where you came.

Each of us in our own way has attempted to become what we already are, proving that we have no idea who we are. So we try harder to be like God, or what we think God is—controlling, judging, proving that we are on the side of good and not evil, but we are missing a key understanding: we already have the thing we seek.

When my two oldest boys were toddlers, we lived in Memphis, Tennessee. We went to Peabody Park to play like we often did on beautiful days. My friend met us with her two kids, Jac and Charis. Charis was barely crawling and Jac was a busy one-year-old boy. He was so busy that he fell sound asleep in my friend's arms while we were talking. We talked fast knowing our time was short and we were trying to catch up on everything. We were also toddler moms, meaning we were sleep deprived and likely socially awkward. Uninterrupted time to talk was rare. By some miracle, my boys, Jaden and Hudson were off playing for longer than usual and our conversation deepened by the minute.

All of a sudden my friend looked up and shouted, "Oh my gosh, where's Jac?"

I had not been paying that much attention but now I zoned in like a momma bear aware that there may be a threat. I see Jaden. I see Hudson, but no Jac.

We went from nonchalant to frantic in a matter of split seconds and began searching every corner of the park for what seemed like fifteen minutes but was probably only two.

We huddled back together having had no luck finding a third little boy as we were running around to find Jac who was still in his mom's arms. We had searched for him, with him right beside us the whole time. We would have never found him scanning the distance…because he was already right there in our arms. It's embarrassing, but somehow we all overlooked him right there beside us, literally with us.

It's a modern story of what Eve experienced in the garden. She went looking for the very thing she already had a hold of—being created in the image of

God. Her pursuit of it "out there" in the distance as if it was out there would never work because it wasn't out there and what she was looking for certainly wouldn't be found by eating from the God-tree. She pursued what she didn't know she already had and took on what she never wanted: what only God can do—judge well.

Every threat you face is some form of judgment that we have dressed up in order to buy the narrative that it's ours to judge. We judge ourselves and then try to fix what we have deemed broken or lacking. We judge others in turn and double down on fixing ourselves to not ever turn out like them. We judge God, often silently, and decide what is truth apart from the creative tools of experience we were given to know God. We exchange the gift of life we were given, humanity, for the burden we were not given, being God. And thus we are threatened by our lack—our utter inability to be God—which we will never be…all the while negating the fact that we were made to be humans in God's image, which we are.

It's time to exchange a life of attempting the impossible, being God, for the gift of life: you're made in the image of God, free to be exactly that: image bearers by birthright.

That tape that's on repeat in your head tells you to doubt yourself. That narrative about never really being lovable and ultimately ending up alone or discovered as a farce. That subtle whisper telling you to hold back your real heart so people will accept your more inline offering. Every should, ought, and must that came from a place other than freedom—each and every one of them is a safety net protecting us from dealing with the thing that actually intimidates us: our own power.

You might be seriously questioning me at this point…We like fear, shame, and insecurity? They feel so bad and they get so old! All the old tapes playing in our head—yuck!

True! But we hold onto them and play the game because they offer us something: avoidance of the immense power we have been given simply by the unique and beautiful way we were made.

The tapes play because we are comfortable, on some level, with them. If we cannot see it, we will not stop it. This book is about seeing and believing what's real about yourself and the world around you. When you are able to see, you can accept, awaken to what is real, and find what we'll call the "comfortable threats" that were protecting you from your very own creative life of abundance and authority.

The story of Genesis 1–3 is about what it is to be a human. Created. Connected. Vibrant. Abundant. In the Image of God. With God. Provided for. Given Authority. Blessed. Free to embrace what is a distinct departure from human addiction to what should be.

Eve demonstrates that humans are most threatened by the radical goodness of what is and, even in Eden's luscious garden, she chooses to eat the fruit of "should be" rather than live in the reality of what is. There's no blame being tossed her way here. I see myself in her, and I'm grateful for the story that helps me understand my own life journey into maturity.

I should be like God. Do you see the embedded threat in that simple thought? I should be (unsaid: I'm not) like God. So I will eat the fruit of the tree where I can be like God and know for myself good from evil. I will be like God.

The issue is twofold: Eve already was like God and Eve was not God.

The tree symbolizes what we do as humans; we forget who we are, attempting to be what we are not. We are chasing our own tails, desperate to get what we already have. This pursuit is an illusion that will keep us in a constant state of fighting, freezing, or fleeing. On a good day, we'll fight: fight for what's right, battle our issues and others if need be. At regular intervals, we'll feel stuck and take some stutter steps and on a bad day, we will run away, retreat, or completely divest. I don't actually think any of these are better than the other. They are all a form of humans doing what humans are not actually designed to do: be God.

Instead, we are children of God. You never have been anything else other than that. It's impossible to exist and be anything less than a child of God, and hear me closely on this one: *made in God's image already.*

The thing we seek, to be like God, is the thing we already had at the beginning: a spitting image. Child status.

This is why the first-century Jewish Rabbi, Yeshua, tells us that we cannot enter his Father's kingdom if we cannot become a child.

Why must we become it, because we are it. We cannot enter falsely. The "not entering" is in direct proportion to the not embracing reality. If a child does not think they can be a child and acts as a parent, they miss crucial personal development milestones. They are a child but think they must be an adult. They are scared of what they are because circumstances and mental assumptions have said: though you are a child, you are not safe being one. Be an adult and you will be safe.

The problem is, they are still a child with all the needs, desires, and dreams that come with childhood. Shoving those to the side may work in many ways but it will not allow them to be the thing that they are: a child.

This is my story. This is your story. This is our human story—our human journey. There is only one.

We are most deeply threatened by what already is. We are far more threatened by our magnificence than we are by our insignificance. It seems to require too little in exchange for what is so great. It merely requires a stroll in the garden enjoying a good conversation with our Maker.

The garden conversation is enough. Being created in the image of God is real, unavoidable, and inescapable. You will always be naked beneath those layers of fig leaves.

The story of our beginning as humans perfectly tells the tale—we were created with everything we needed. Lacking nothing. Unafraid. Nothing to hide. In the garden, walking and talking with God. Made distinctly in the image of the very Gods who birthed us from their love dance. The chaos, the word, and the breath created humans in their image—female and male—they were very good.

But as the story goes, the age-old threat to humans did not turn out to be that they were lacking in goodness, without value or needing to hide anything—the threat actually showed up in the form of acceptance, awareness, and abundance.

Dismantling the threats will involve acceptance of what is real, awareness of what is real and abundant experience of what is real. These tools for dismantling what threatens us are processed in the mind but deeply integrated and connected to every other part of your life and the world around you. The best tools for dismantling threats will not show up for you like they are the best. They will feel too easy, fun, and enjoyable for you, at first, to register them as powerful. This is how you will know you are on the right track: it will not be as difficult as you imagined!

Let's practice discovering what is real. Take up to one minute to write out your train of thought, however those thoughts may come to you. Set a timer. Don't take less than fifteen seconds or more than one minute and you can write down anything. The only wrong way to do this is to not write down what comes to mind.

For example, if you can't think of anything, that is what your mind is thinking, so write it out very simply: "I can't think of anything. Why am I doing this? I need to call the pharmacy. Oh shit, I'm distracted, what am I supposed to be doing?"

Train of thought is what we are going for. The more detailed the better, so if you think in little pictures and movies, put that down.

For example, if while thinking about not thinking of anything, there's a picture in your mind of say a blank paper or blank computer screen—write that down too—describe it. Or if when the thought of calling the pharmacy pops into your mind, go ahead and describe how it popped. Were you picturing yourself calling and pressing the number for the prescription? Put that down. Were you imagining yourself driving through the pharmacy pick-up line (I am literally picturing this for myself right now; it's the San Antonio Broadway Central Market parking garage pharmacy drive-through—they have this odd shooter for the prescriptions that sticks out in lane two). The depth is in the details here, so spend less time not writing and more time being detailed about whatever it is that comes to mind.

Include any feelings that you feel currently, in the present. Also, include any feelings that arise that might be associated with whatever comes to mind.

For example, if I hate driving through the pharmacy pick-up line, I might all of a sudden have the remembrance feeling of dread. I don't actually dread the drive-through, but I do immediately think of the feeling that I'd like to go wander around Central Market if I have time to find a few unique and hard-to-find food products, especially at Christmas.

Our brains process with words, but far beyond words. In a split second, we can visualize a little brain movie, feel, intuit, have a sense of meaning, string together words and interpretations or stories that use many senses to weave together "thinking"—and it all takes just a moment. It takes much longer to describe it in words and pictures on paper than it does to think about it.

Grab a piece of paper or use the space below, set your timer for a minute, and don't take longer than that. Now write whatever accurately describes your thought life for the next sixty seconds. Good, bad, ugly, and everything in between is totally fine—this is not a test. You don't have to share it with anyone. This is solely to help you think about the way you think, how things come to your brain, and how you process it. You will think and process very similarly to me and everyone else but it will also be unique to you. You might think in feelings first more often than I do and that's worth noting. You might constantly be thinking in pictures, then come to the words, then the feelings, and then a mix of all at the same time. You might think in sentences and words as a default weaving through pictures, movies, and feelings at times. Notice the unique way you think your thoughts as they come and as you look back on what you write. Okay, go!

Sixty-Second Brain Dump:

Look back at the way you just thought…

What do you notice?

How did your thoughts come most frequently? Picture? Mind-movie?
Feeling? Word? Sentences? A big swirl?

Great, end this simple practice by noticing if you are judging what came up and let that go. This is a practice not an evaluation and part of the practice is to release yourself from your own personal judgments, even the subtlest ones. Say yes to *noticing* and release yourself from any pressure to judge whether you think you're right or not.

Genesis 1 and 2 lays out the flow of creation that was there in the beginning and will never cease. It's where we came from, what we forgot, what we struggle to discover, and all we'll come to know as home in good time.

In the beginning, everything you needed to *experience* what's real in life was laid out. Not everything you need to *know*. *Everything you need to experience*. It is engageable: we can see it, hear it, feel it, and practice it. Better said, we can jump into the flow of the river that began it all, the water's fine. You are already naturally doing this and a simple 60 second brain dump will show you your own internal communication practices. It will show you how you are interpreting what you experience. Not only is it safe for you to express these things, it's essential to express them so you can become aware of them. Once you are aware, you can choose and transform them - before you are aware, you are limited by them. The simple practices of *Mind Alchemy* will help you discover your life's flow and it begins with becoming aware of the language of your inner dialogue.

My Story—

BLACK HOLES AND BRIGHT LIGHTS

How I Learned Mind Alchemy

We come into the world without language but we are very much aware. Our earliest memories, even from the womb, dramatically shape the lives we live decades later but because they are pre-verbal, we are often unaware of the very things we were wide awake to and aware of in our infancy.

Mind alchemy is both a process of going back to reclaim past awareness, and the process of waking up to what shapes us so profoundly, and mind alchemy is about the present-future state of our lives. We are in the present, which is the farthest we will ever go into the future (present-future state). My intention is that *Mind Alchemy* helps you rediscover what you never knew you knew and empowers you to get into the flow of your life through simple practices that are not difficult. I may have learned some of them the hard way but that doesn't mean you have to. I imagine there is deep learning you too have done the hard way—the practices in this book will help you mine that wisdom and turn it into practical life-giving exercises you too can share.

The part of my story I want to share with you begins in the womb. I know we don't really remember our womb life, but deep down we do. Finding out what I felt then is part of the alchemy that has freed me to become myself today.

In the womb, I was keenly aware of my mom. Though I didn't have words yet, it didn't require too much intuition to know this about her from the start: she was broken. I felt the conflict within her and of course, I wore it for much of my life as if it was passed in the DNA, but it wasn't. I now know it was hers and I wore it like a warm winter jacket. I branded the inner turmoil from the inside of her onto the inside of me: elated shame. Elated to be alive, but terrified that I should in all my guilt, die.

I felt the threat of death at an early age—imagine scissors coming at you from the outside of your small cocoon causing you to curl up tightly away from the opening. This was the picture that first came to mind as I thought about my womb life: dark, confusing, scary, and threatening. How do I know this? That will make sense in a minute.

My earliest interpretations of life were these: the world is not a safe place, my caretaker is fragile, and so I must be easy and good so I don't die. If I'm not easy, this woman will break. I had no idea then that the voice whispering in my ear was shame. Deeply seeded, understandable generational shame. It took on the sound of my own voice in the form of my own thoughts reverberating in my own mind so, also understandably, I thought it was me.

Since I was curled up so high in the womb, I was extracted with forceps—they caught my mouth causing nerve damage to my lip—sometimes you can still see it when I smile.

I, Cayce Claire Yates, begrudgingly entered the world, but my parents were delighted! I would be the only pregnancy that would stick for them despite wanting five kids. Both in their second marriage and nearly forty, they were simply elated to have me.

I was hospitalized at three months old for a week with a very high fever—the doctors told my aunt who was keeping me not to tell my parents who were in Europe: "She'll either be dead by the time they get back or she'll be just fine," he said. I survived and I got busy being easy. I was an easy baby, toddler, and grade schooler. After terrible marriages, my parents found a deep love in each other. I was the embodiment of redemption for both of their lives as well as the target for all their maternal and paternal energy. This was both lovely and overwhelming.

My tendency to be easy, quiet, and blend in was reinforced dramatically by what is my very first actual memory—I was young, I'm guessing I was about eighteen months to three years old. On a regular check-up at the pediatrician's office, the doctor placed himself and me in an area apart from my mom and he sexually abused me under the guise of a check-up. The memory is still in slow motion for me, probably because I was in shock. I felt extremely violated but didn't have any words for it and zero voice—I lay there stunned and silent. I was confused because to my young self, this man was supposed to be trustworthy—he was doing something to "help" me. It felt so wrong, but I forced an interpretation that I must be wrong and he must be right. My world started spinning and getting very small. It's as if there was a part of me that fell back into myself and then into a dark hole on that doctor's table—I was so unprepared for what was happening to me that whatever parts of me were scrambling to make meaning decided it was best to put this memory in the *far back* of my brain so that I could come out of the stunned silence and back into my life.

This experience, though consciously forgotten for a season, would shape much of my life. I spoke very little and had constant anxiety at a young age around anyone new—especially older men. "She's so shy," people would comment to my mom. "What a pretty, small, and quiet child." I loved people and got lost in my imagination about all the grand things of life, but when it came to actually interacting with people, I was terrified, and anxiety was my constant companion. I always found the safest people in the room to talk with, if anyone at all.

My mom was a perfectionist, one who could lose her temper easily, who had so much shame from her own story that connection was difficult at that point in her life, and self-loathing was always just under the surface.

There *are* moments I remember in my childhood when I felt completely free and full of life, usually by myself because I did not feel comfortable being seen. *By myself,* you could find me dancing for hours to Amy Grant's first cassette tape featuring two songs: "Father's Eyes" and "El Shaddai" or singing really loudly with Garth Brooks.

If you could peel back my chest, you'd see my heart jump for joy around art supplies of any kind, especially paint—the consistency and unlimited options of what could happen with it thrilled me. At the same time, I did not think I was an artist and I didn't know how to use the materials so I discounted the option pretty early on.

Genuine contemplation of faith was an early practice. I had a million questions about God to ponder and I did. I also had some very real experiences of God's presence. I have always felt at home with God, albeit many times disconnected, shamed, and confused by religion and religious leaders.

I experienced a miracle when I was six years old. I had a recurring nightmare filled with the shame and trauma of what had happened to me with the doctor. Still today I can remember the dream well. Now the dream makes a lot of sense considering what happened to me as a toddler but at the time, it simply terrorized me. I couldn't speak when I'd wake from it—I would just shake. My mom knew something was happening but I would never tell her the contents of my dream. Over and over I had the dream.

One night she said, "Cayce, why don't we ask Jesus to take that bad dream away?"

She prayed a very simple prayer and I never had that dream ever again. In fact, I never had another nightmare again. I started having dreams that were vibrant and full of life. I felt connected to God through my dreams. Something transformed for me, and those old memories of trauma were held even more at bay.

After that, I began to come out of my shell—the part of me that really loves being with people woke up and I went from being the very quiet, good girl to the one who was friends with everyone. I was a popular kid who everyone was okay with from about third grade on. I had fun with people and loved being included in whatever was happening.

Growing up, I worked really hard to be a safe space because that's how I learned to navigate life—with that came all kinds of confessions from friends. I used to think that I just happened to have people in my world who also had experienced early sexual trauma, that somehow we were all drawn to each other. Maybe so, but maybe that kind of thing is just all too prevalent. Either way, I was very aware of how ashamed and confused we all were by it. Understandably, we all worked hard to hide it. We also all thought it was our fault, which was more evidence of how bad we were from the beginning. (An aside: as a mom, it's so hard to look at my kids and imagine how they could ever shame or blame themselves the way I did as a kid, I pray they don't, but when you are the kid going through it, it all seems just very natural and normal because it's all you know. Then pile on a theology that tells you how you are born broken and separated from God because of something big called sin nature, and viola—yes, you are to blame, you think to yourself; it all just fits and makes sense. Until it doesn't. The problem is, what I believed about myself wasn't true. The false narratives will break down eventually, thank God).

I learned to be a good listener and therefore, a peacemaker (little did I know this service to the world was all about me and making me feel at peace, but at that time I just thought it was what I was supposed to do). I studied enough to be near the top of my class but never at the very top because that would draw too much attention. I played every sport I could and was always a good player in practice where there was no pressure, but I choked in games because games brought with them two things I didn't like: pressure to perform and eyes on me.

Middle school and high school were fun for me—I wasn't as terrified as I had been for the first decade of my life. I traveled all over the world with my parents, the benefit of being an only child to older parents. They were ready to enjoy their life and they took me with them! I think it's for this reason that I feel most at home when I get to travel often. I love being immersed in different cultures, and staying in one place for very long periods is not something that has ever interested me.

I was drawn to authentic adults who seemed to me to have a faith life that was real to them. This mattered to me because I was around so many people who were professing Christians and praying a lot. I mean a lot. At a small evangelical Christian school, you pray before a test and before a sports game. You pray when someone is in the hospital, and you pray when someone has a hangnail. It's nice, it doesn't always feel authentic or connected to real life, real questions, and present needs for connection. I didn't know how to explain why, but it made me tired and disheartened. I picked up a lot of beauty, Bible, but also, baggage from my school. I interpreted much that was taught to me through a lens of shame. Unfortunately, that shame was only reinforced by much of what I experienced with other Christians. Lots of good intentions. Lots of hiding.

The God I talked to often and dreamed with at night was not at all like the one I was trying to make sense of that was talked about in school. I'll spare you the details but you should know that much of the work I do now comes directly from my frustration with a theology that thrives on shoulds and oughts and doles out condemnation rather than authentic connection and freedom. I studied the Bible since I could read because that's what I was told I should do—that's the silver lining of my evangelical upbringing, despite lots of misinterpretation and bias—the Bible is the Bible and it's really beautiful. I've studied in Israel six different times, a privilege I never want to take for granted. As a kid, my dream job was to be a missionary (ala Amy Carmichael), a writer (think Oswald Chambers and Andrew Murray) and a stockbroker just like my dad. I pretty much wanted to be anyone other than me.

I felt called and compelled to a life of "serving God." Today that phrase makes me chuckle because it's not at all how I feel about my life. I enjoy my relationship with God so much and it's a delight to do what I do—make a connection with God simple and practicable for others without the theological arguments that I was immersed in from age six to thirty. Healing happens all the time and I know how to help people find it if they are truly interested in that. I no longer view it as serving God but as a really great time with my favorite people in the world!

I've jumped ahead—a quick catch-up: I attended Rhodes College in Memphis, Tennessee. I met Joel Harris there. We dated while we both also traveled in opposite directions around the globe. I did not plan to get married early. I wanted to travel the world for a while before something like that, but I was also in love with Joel, and we decided we could travel together. That is not exactly what happened for many reasons. Every time we tried, life offered us opportunities that lured us back into a less exotic version of adventure. Instead of India after we married, we stuck to Memphis and instead of South Africa like we planned three years later, we made a detour to San Antonio for Joel's work in education.

I was up to three things early in our marriage:

1. I learned about Christian inner healing. I didn't know if I would ever become a practitioner but I knew I desperately needed it. This is how I know what little Cayce in the womb felt and interpreted. I have all kinds of crazy stories but here's a small example: in one of my first sessions, God brought to mind a picture of the womb and showed me how I was feeling and why. The why took the form of this picture of scissors coming at me in the womb. I thought I was losing my mind and making crazy stuff up in this session but I went with it. As I "remembered" this early experience, Jesus showed up and closed the scissors with His gentle hands. He then filled the dark cold memory with light. The womb turned from midnight to noon in a moment, and He told me that I wasn't going to die. He told me that He would be with me always and that I was welcome in the world.

    Whether I made it up or not, this was hugely relieving for me to hear because it explained so much of the angst I felt my entire life. About a year later, I told my mom about the experience and she broke down sobbing. She then told me what she had only told one other living soul. She had been date raped after college. Her story is hers to tell, but her anger, guilt, and shame festered for years. She felt so much shame, especially when she was pregnant with me. This was the beginning of a whole new relationship with my mom. She ended up getting healing prayer too and spent hours dealing with the shame and rage she felt. She's now a different woman than I grew up with.

2. I started a photography business. I didn't like it that much because I spent too much time processing behind a computer screen. But I did enjoy the people and creative process.

3. I got pregnant six months into our marriage.

Jaden was followed by a miscarriage and then ten months later came Hudson. Twenty-four months later, my daughter Claire burst into our world. The kids were amazing, I loved being a mom to infants and yes, it was joyful chaos for most of their early years of life.

Now living in San Antonio, Joel and I began living very separate lives—he worked, a lot. I worked as much as I could while also coordinating everything for three toddlers. When Claire was born I quit photography and opened a bridesmaid's dress store in San Antonio and in Austin with my best friend Kim. I helped start an inner healing prayer ministry and women's ministry for Alamo Heights United Methodist Church. I ended up spending less time selling dresses and more time talking to the brides and helping them process where they were in life. It's hard to make good money in small shop retail. I decided that if I ever had a business again we would need to be able to mark things up at least ten times their cost for it to be worth it—plus I would rather just meet with people anyway. A sudden move to Hawaii ended my ownership stake in Bella Bridesmaid.

Hawaii was amazing for three months, and then I fell into the deepest depression of my life. I can see now that so much of my identity was wrapped up in what kind of healing and help I could offer to people that my winning strategy (thank you to Tracy Goss for that language and understanding) must have just freaked out when I had no one to help. I wasn't "serving God" anymore, and I didn't know who I was or what I wanted. For six months I felt like I was in a black lockbox and couldn't find the handle to get out. I went into this black hole in a day and I also came out in a day. There was a lot of dialogue between me and God and my journal that day, but as I remember it, my strongest words to God were, "Motherfucker where the hell are you?" There were more words, I had broken down completely—but on that day, I broke through—back into joy and into life again.

Something interesting happened to me during that six-month lockbox: *nothing* —worked—all my old tools—worship, prayer, talking it through with friends, counseling, journaling, and exercising. I would go to the beach, put my feet in the water, feel the waves hit them, and just breathe. It was all I knew to do. One thing worked and I found it by what seemed at the time to be an accident. I started something new. I enrolled in an oil painting course through the University of Manoa. This class led to a world-renowned artist who I painted with all over the island multiple times a week.

The only time I felt like myself and found relief from the extreme depression I was experiencing was when I painted. Everything else faded away, including time, sadness, and discomfort. I was completely enthralled. This was unexpected and unintended. I met the most amazing people painting on the beaches of Oahu. It's one of my favorite things about my life thus far.

We thought we were done having babies and we were shocked to find out we were pregnant again. This may have added to my depression, but what actually happened was that Yates was the burst of bright light that completely transformed the memory of a dark season. Yates was and still is *joy* embodied. He made us want to have a fifth—all our kids did really—we already had four. Out of necessity we had given up on the illusion of control, and so we just decided to keep going and to enjoy the heck out of them.

When our first was born, a plumber came to the house, looked at me intently, and said, "You know that Jesus broke the curse of pain in childbirth don't you? You don't have to have pain in childbirth." This was ballsy because he didn't know me from Adam. A newly pregnant mom that I was, that sounded too good to be true, but also something I would be interested in. I believed it could happen and I sure wanted it to. It did not happen. I was in pain with a capital "P."

I had all my babies in bathtubs at home or in a birth center. Yes, I am a little brave, but more than that I disconnected from my body at an early age so my pain tolerance was extremely high. Why am I telling you this? Well unexpectedly, Yates, our Hawaii baby came with zero pain. I did indeed experience a pain-free childbirth and it was glorious. I used much of what you'll learn in this book during his birth and what happened to me during his birth was full of vision, joy, and elation. It can happen.

Fast forward to our fifth baby, Lee, and the story is much different. On February 19, 2017, San Antonio went on a tornado-warning lockdown—a couple of tornadoes tore through Oak Park, the neighborhood we lived in, hitting our home and trashing the acre of land we had just purchased.

Thankfully we were not there. We were driving to the birth center to give birth to Lee. The power was out all around us, our building was somehow the only one on the block with power. The tornado outside felt like it was inside—Lee was having trouble. His heart rate sank dangerously low—we're talking to thirty. I was barely in labor, only six to seven centimeters dilated, and my midwife looked at us.

With clear instructions, she said, "Joel, you call an ambulance. Cayce, I'm so sorry to ask you to do this but you can do it (she had attended Claire and Yates's births). You have to push this baby out now."

She told me later that she had never been more scared for a baby or a mom, but since she had been with me through the two prior births, she took a risk by asking me to push rather than wait for the ambulance. Six minutes later, precious Lee was out and resuscitated. I didn't think much about what my body had just done but for the first time in my life, my body would find "words" to tell me that it was not okay in the years to come.

After Lee was born, my husband Joel attended a program in New York City called Executive Reinvention Program led by a woman and friend named Tracy Goss. Tracy led the group through a deep dive into understanding their default way of being in life which she calls "winning strategy." This was the beginning of a whole new season for us in so many ways. We didn't even know that our winning strategies were keeping us from the deep connection we wanted with each other. We had buried our individual desires and our desires as a couple beneath many amazing things: our kids, our jobs, and our community. It was time to uncover them.

One simple question transformed the trajectory of our lives, "What do you really really want?" I attended the same program six months after Joel and got in touch with what I wanted. It was always there, but I was skilled at ignoring it, belittling it, or saving it for later. For the first time in a long time, Joel and I decided that we were unstoppably committed to integrating our lives. We had been married and busy for fourteen years. We were tired of running hard in separate but supportive directions and had enough. This decision was right on time. I have needed Joel more than I have been comfortable with in the past five years because physically my body was breaking down.

I bounced back after the first four births, but the last one was entirely different and it surfaced issues that my body was screaming about. I had not been ready to pay attention until now. After Lee was born, I had to slow down in every way and care for myself. *Mind Alchemy* was born from this slowdown. As soon as my body slowed down, so much of what had been forming in me for the past four decades coalesced. What you read here is integrated into an experience called The One Journey that we offer people for seven days on a little island off the coast of Texas.

It's the best work I've ever done and I enjoy every minute of it. This is one of the many gifts that the past five years of slowing down have given me. The gift of physical weakness has also been that I have been forced to focus on the long game of caring for my own skin and bones, something that, in my winning strategy, I had rejected doing for the early part of my life.

In March 2020, Yates, our fourth kiddo who was six years old at the time, had a horrific accident in Colorado while sledding on the ski slope. He broke his face in eighty places. He could have, some would say "should" have, died. He is a complete miracle. So much could have gone wrong that didn't. They originally thought we could be in the hospital for weeks. We spent only four days in the hospital and no one could believe how Yates healed right before our eyes. This was the week the world shut down for COVID. Due to the emergency situation we were in, I had ten different doctors talking very close to my face and they weren't wearing face masks. Two weeks later, I developed a serious case of COVID—one of the first in our community.

Because of my compromised state, I got it bad. Forty days of fever, feeling like glass was shattering in my lungs, and head and neck pain with no reprieve. I experienced another miracle that kept me out of the hospital which is very good because, at that point, they put you immediately on a ventilator—not a place anyone wanted to be.

I surrendered. I was never in control but now, I keenly knew it. I could do nothing else but let go. I learned a skill I never had access to before. I learned to release myself into a deep state of restful meditation to get out of pain rather than numbing and ignoring my body. COVID broke something in me. I let go of work responsibilities, of needing to be the primary caregiver to our kids, of feeling guilt and shame for not being present in our family, of the anxiety that surrounded all things COVID, and I just focused on caring for my body.

In May I was reunited with my family and we spent as much time on the Texas coast as possible. It was healing to breathe the ocean air and walk the beach. Joel and the kids surfed every day. It was *so great* that we decided to move there. Now we straddle two cities and have a few different jobs, but we have shrunk our world in order to have more quality time as a family. It worked and we are exactly where we want to be.

There's another theme of my life. My first actual memories may have been tragic and disorienting, but it didn't stop the creation of thousands of magical memories that followed. One of the earliest is this, stepping out of a small plane—my dad's buddy's—and onto a strip of concrete by the Texas Gulf Coast. I was three and my dad carried me on his shoulders off the plane, into an old Silverado Chevy Suburban, and whisked me to the condos he and his buddy were building for the serious fishermen of Texas. These were not condos for fancy beach tourists. These were in the hottest location (and I say that in jest as nothing has ever been "hot" in this sleepy fishing village) in the middle of a very small town called Port Mansfield, Texas, right where the town met the expansive opening to the bay. We spent the summers of my childhood there and visited as often as possible throughout the school year. My best memories of traveling have always centered on the beach and the ocean. I felt at home if I was on a boat, no matter the size, surrounded by water. In college when looking at study abroad options, I of course opted for the floating school, Semester at Sea.

One day, I was driving and the gentle nudge of God's spirit whispered, "Forgive the doctor."

"But God, I have, many times."

"Forgive him again, for you."

The very next day he showed up unexpectedly. I wish I could say it was for healing but it was for our fundraiser. That day from the stage in front of 600 people, I shared part of my story of healing from abuse. I haven't seen him since but I could breathe in front of him and even look at him with forgiveness and even with empathy.

During those forty days of my first bout with COVID, I woke from a dream in this quiet whisper, "Cayce, I didn't make you for the hospital, I made you for the beach." This one word spoke volumes to my soul as someone who not only had been in and out of the hospital with various illnesses but as someone who naturally gravitated to the helping work of hospitals.

For a season through my job with Christ Healing Center (we later changed the name to ONE), my area of care was the hospital ministry—praying with and for doctors, patients, and family of the hospitalized. This was a fuller expression of what I had always thought was "my role" in life—to be there when people were hurting—emotionally, physically, spiritually—I was there. It was also slowly killing me.

Though I have experienced a few black holes in my life, I am certain of one thing—I am not one. The little girl in that womb may have thought she was in the dark for a time, but she never really was. She was always pure light because her Source is pure light. The little girl on the doctor's table went into a dark cave that day. It was so dark that she thought she might have died but she did not. She's been resurrected, and though she remembers the table and the cave, she is no longer there. She moves freely now just like the Breath of God that is in her.

There's an ancient poem about the seven stages of a woman's life. First, she is a daughter, then a maiden, then she's a creator. The final stage, after a few others, is a healer. I skipped some stages and I jumped to healer because I desperately needed healing, but now I am going back. There are pieces of my personhood that I want to pick up. Much, if not all of this book comes from that journey.

The practice doesn't require any previous knowledge or set of beliefs for you to engage with it. You don't need to believe anything specific about life or God, even though the practices will help you engage in conversation with God. Again, try it out and see how it works first *before* trying to define what you think. We can think anything, but what is true remains true regardless of what we think about it. At the same time, what we think is powerful enough to shape our experiences and cause them to appear like reality. If you are willing to let go of needing to define things for a moment, embrace the practices, then use honest language to describe them, you'll have more success in the long run with every area of your life.

The practices of Mind Alchemy are rooted in the story of our beginnings in Genesis.

The beginning of the story is a perfect invitation for all the beginners among us. *In the beginning, God created…* this story holds space for us to begin with God. New life and new beginnings are the seedbed of the creative.

Three Foundational Practices

The basics of mind alchemy are these three simple practices:

1. Show up honest to your own story (at the very least, be honest with yourself).

2. Be willing to practice a dialogue in your thought life.

3. Notice what you notice.

Showing up honest will take the form of questions and descriptions. Being willing to practice dialogue means you start to notice the different conversations and are willing to shift the "many" into just a few. Noticing what you notice is being willing to think about the way you think while describing the landscape of your mind. These three practices will show up in different ways throughout this book, and the more you practice them, the more they will mean to you.

About Threats—

DEEP BREATHS, DEEP CARES,
DEEP CONVERSATIONS

When I was six years old I remember talking to God. Then, it was the way I processed thoughts late into the night. I imagine I'm not the only kid who had a natural curiosity and practice of quiet mental conversations with their concept of "God." It never stopped for me. The interest, engagement, and practice of mind conversations with God were a constant in a world of variables. Through each of my short-lived interests, throughout childhood, teens, and into my young adulthood, I knew I could and would always find a home in that built-in mind space where I could talk to God. It's been the saving grace of my life. This doesn't mean I always felt clear on the concept of God. It doesn't mean I always felt secure or like God was really there. But it does mean I kept coming back to a conversation with God that was *near* and that's the foundation for where we'll start. If there's something I've known for the majority of my life it's that God is near.

We all have *something* we do or know or practice intuitively that we don't realize is unique to us because it's so normal. Normal, that is for us, but not necessarily for everyone else. There are things each of us do throughout our lives and we think nothing of it because it's driven by such an innate intelligence. Talking with God is mine. It took me twenty years to truly value what

I'd learned through the practice in a way that would allow me to share it with others. Another twenty to value it enough to write about it. Looking back, there's so much I've been unsure of in my life. So much that I've discovered the roundabout way or by the very real teacher of trial and error. So much of our lives truly only make some sense looking back. What I share in this book comes from that place: *looking back*, this is the constant of my life that makes sense. Not everything in my life is like that. Some things make less sense now as I look back. There are question marks and fond memories, lost memories, and threads of stories. Some things are too easily forgotten or overlooked, and others are ingrained as if they happened yesterday. This concept I'll guide you to engage, for me, cannot be avoided, overlooked, forgotten, buried, or denied. It's not just part of my path, it is my path. Denial is futile. Rejection is ridiculous. All there is to do is to walk it and to share the beauty of it with friends.

I'm curious about what path you're walking. What path have you been walking since the very beginning? I wonder what has driven you. What has driven you from the very beginning from your core? Not to be crass right at the beginning of this book, but the familiarly awkward phrase from my childhood that pops in my mind here to express how I feel about this is: I'll show you mine if you show me yours. The truth about me is that as a kid I hated that statement. If someone said it to me I would have bolted.

The imagery and feelings, as childish and awkward as they might sound, are actually a perfect analogy for this bigger thing I'm talking about—the thing in your life that you may feel very naked sharing about, but it's part of you and it's actually really beautiful, good, and life-giving. It's worth sharing, at the right time when you are ready. The sharing can take so many different forms, but it will always have this commonality: it will be creative and artistic. Notice I didn't say "artsy"—not having to do with what you might think of as art. No, I mean it in a much more elemental way: what comes from you when you are willing to show up honest and honor who you really are—the path you have discovered that you are on. That kind of sharing will always create, and *that creation* will be art. It will be full of life and that life will be transmittable. It won't shut down. It will enliven just by the nature of the integrity of what is being shared not because you have set out to create art. When you do create something you want to share, please don't hesitate to share it with me. I look forward to seeing and hearing from you.

Here's mine…

Mind Alchemy comes from thirty-two years of practice and piecing together books, talks, and thoughts that have fascinated me about brain science, God, and interpersonal growth dynamics—twenty of those years in the small-niched world of Jesus-centric inner healing. This is my attempt at writing the book I wish I had read in my late teens or early twenties. Once I started writing, re-writing, and procrastinating, this book took five years to complete and transformed from one thing into an entirely other thing. The greatest challenge I had was how to make this practical and engageable for everyone. That is my intent, that regardless of your background culturally, spiritually, politically, ideologically—that this book can be of value to you *practically*. If a book can't be put into practice in your real-world life, I'm not sure it is worth the cost unless it's a great storybook—stories are always worth it. But a nonfiction on spirituality? It better be helpful!

Here's my intent:

I want this book to be simple enough to be engaged and complex enough to truly open a whole new world for you in your daily life. If you both read and engage the practices of this book, it will undoubtedly take you to a deeper and fuller experience of your life. I write with the desire that *Mind Alchemy* is a book that you can return to and find deeper levels of engagement and insight because what inspires you today will be different from what inspires you in the future, and what threatens you today shows up much differently than it did ten years ago.

Care Surfaces What Threatens You

Our family is a team-sports family. When the kids were little, we told them they could only play one team sport at a time, and they better really like it because with five kids we are not the type of parents who are trying to fill a schedule. We are the ones trying to make seven people's schedules somehow work together—multiple sports teams per person just doesn't work for us.

If you are a Harris kid, growing up there are things you're just not gonna get, like a consistent schedule or a generally quiet home. We moved a lot (to fit the needs of our growing family, and as my dad would say, nomadism is in the genes). Our kids haven't hesitated to tell us they would not do that to their kids—our oldest says he'll live in one place and never move. We'll see.

They will likely make different and infinitely better choices on their own journey, and we are not the perfect parents, so there will be plenty of growth areas for them to work out on their own healing journey. Having said that, there's one thing not one of our kids lacks: passion. If you know my husband and me, this won't surprise you. We might appear calm about it, but we're intense, trust me. We care. We have birthed five strong, passionate, and focused individuals. They care. Their personalities express it differently but their lives say this, "If I'm into it, I'm intensely into it."

One is passionate about basketball, people, and getting it right for the sake of integrity. Another is passionate about time alone, jazz, justice, fishing, hunting, and golf. One is so passionate about surfing that he'd dream about it and wake up weeping at age seven because he wasn't living near the ocean (yet). One is the best kind of intense friend, fiercely competitive, and passionately committed to a good joke. Another really cares about learning and school, playing video games, and fighting to be heard and seen—passion is nothing if not the best kind of intensity.

Passion works in two directions: toward desired behavior and against it. When I say "against" it, I'm not talking about intent or desire but it works through function. Function is how it actually operates and works. Why does beginner's luck happen? Because there's no passion, concern, or real level of care for success. So the way passion can actually work "against" success does not yet exist. What happens when we start to care? What happens when we move toward something that we really want and care about? Sooner or later our positive passion for a thing also surfaces a deeper shared human experience: the fear that we could lose it all, fail, not achieve, not experience, mess up, miss out on, hurt, or sabotage the very thing we so desperately want.

A simple example of how it works is basketball.

For years our kids who played ball practiced and worked hard on and off the court to be able to play this game on teams. They cared. Their care-filled practice produced results. Year after year they experienced success, meaning that their physical practice paid off. They got better, more experienced, and more coordinated.

At a certain point, it becomes clear that physical agility and improvement are not *all* that's needed. This point comes after an indefinite amount of time and care has been invested into a passion. This point also is reached quicker by success in said passionate pursuit. This "point" is the point where one's passion can work against further success. Because of the passion factor, care becomes a roadblock to further success. What kind of success am I talking about? Mastery in execution. Care is the greatest block to the authentic execution of mastery because it surfaces so much more than physical ability. It surfaces the stuff we all deal with—fear, shame, insecurity, dreams, desires, authenticity, and vulnerability. There it all is under the guise of winning a district championship or leading a work team to hit a seemingly unattainable target or taking the next step in a relationship.

Care shows up in all kinds of normal places. Care about getting better. Care about the game. Care about a team. Care about pleasing coaches. Care about what people think. Care about the future and make the best choices. It's complex and not always obvious what we really care about. We aren't always aware that our care has shifted from the original "care" or love of the game to something less important like pleasing a coach or maintaining past great dynamics so that we can avoid feeling shame, but it happens.

Care or passion for the game morphs into a dynamic that works against a person's ability to do well. It's too much care; it's misplaced care. All of a sudden a coordinated high school senior looks like a seventh grader handling the ball. All of a sudden a carefree personality dims behind the pressure of winning, the intense pressure to not make mistakes, and the specter of not achieving future goals. At best, what started out as a fun game becomes mentally, emotionally, and physically draining. At worst, the "work" of passion creates a constant state of stress that's discouraging and depressing. The switch of passion has been flipped, and the electrical current that started the whole thing off, in the beginning, seems to be cut off entirely.

This happens in something as seemingly simple as high school sports, but it's just a picture of what happens to almost everyone at some point around something they care about in life.

This is an incredibly consistent experience in the human journey. So what is it and what can we practice to find the powerful side of passion again and move with the beautiful God-given current we have each been given? Unsure if you have been given this gift? Check your breath. Are you breathing? That is literally the current of life, your life and mine, running through us right now. It says, scientifically and metaphorically, that the spirit is present in your body.

Whose spirit? If you don't know what you think about God, what you can see in your own breath is your own spirit, abiding in the present like waves on the sea. In your inhale, your life is rushing to the shore. In the exhale, the current takes you out into the world around you.

You are here, breathing, alive and connected—whether you know it or not—to the world around you. This is not insignificant. In fact, it's extraordinary, and deep down, you know it. Built into our humanity is a natural curiosity, weight, or care for the importance of being alive. Innately, we ask all the important questions, often very quietly: What is love? Who am I? What is my purpose? How do I serve? Is there a God? What's the meaning of life? Who is my neighbor? Why am I here now? What is death? What happens after death? What matters? Do I matter? Am I good? Am I worth loving?

Think about how the deep questions find their way to the surface of our consciousness whether we want them to or not in seemingly simple things like trying out for a basketball team. At some point, the questions will arise: am I good enough? Do I have what it takes? Do I have something of value to offer? Worth it? Worthy? It may be subtle but the questions are there, and they will surface sooner or later because the questions are built in, and because care causes them to move from invisible to visible. Often this threatens us, but the practices of this book will help you recognize that what shows up as a threat is actually a powerful proposition. If we can get curious enough, we can transform what threatens us into what teaches us, leads us, and causes the kinds of breakdowns that will actually form us into who we really are—magnificent human beings who find their value far beyond what they do or don't do right in a basketball game.

Your passions and desires will surface in what we'll call the shadowland of your desires. What do we do practically to walk through these seasons? What practices will actually move us out of bobbing aimlessly through the positive and negative currents of our passions and into the great flow of our lives as humans?

We'll learn seven. The remainder of this book is built around them and they come from the Creation story in Genesis 1. These are creative practices—not artistic, *creative*. They create something. That's not a grand statement. It's just reality. The reality of your life is that you are a creative being; you cannot avoid it. You are creating your life right now. You may very well be stuck mentally in the past or traumatized and therefore what you are "creating" right now is a re-creation of your traumatized past. Regardless, I promise that you're moving in a current that is creative simply by being alive. This is important to understand as we do these basic practices. Whoever said, "Wherever you go, there you are!" said it in the same vein that I say, "Whatever you do, you are creating." *Can you get present enough to where you are, what you want, and what you're doing to start moving with enjoyment in the act of creation that is your life?* That's the core question of the book. A question I want to help you find answers to that are simple and life-giving regardless of your age, stage, or circumstances in life.

You can engage in these practices right away, and I encourage you to try them all first. Then come back to your favorites and do them again, more often.

The threats we'll look at are common to human type threats. Experiencing them is a normal part of the human experience. While that is true, the deceptive thought that accompanies most of these threats is some version of this sentiment: You're all alone. You're the only one. You're the problem. Sometimes that concern takes different shapes but the underlying emphasis is the same. You'll feel the underlying sense that you're alone and you're likely to get it wrong. So a little warning signal goes off on the inside and the tendency here is often to just hide. The great thing about a book that you are reading alone is that you can make the choice here and now that you're not gonna hide from yourself any longer, even when you feel threatened.

Often, threats in life don't look as dramatic and come across our radar in seemingly small ways: comparison, negative self-talk, low-level anxiety, insecurity, depression, disengagement, feeling withheld, boxed in, stuck, and insignificant.

Here's where you can practice noticing what you notice: pause and take note of how you feel right now. If you could put two to three words or phrases on how your mind feels right now in life, what would you say? If you could put two to three words or phrases on how your body feels right now in life, how would you describe it? What about your spirit or what some call your heart? What words would you use to honestly describe how you feel now? Look back at it; what's a normal feeling? What part of you feels threatened? What part of you needs attention?

Remember, show up honest at least for yourself. Dialogue is your friend. When you express a thought, ask a good follow-up question, for now to yourself is fine, but in the next chapter, we'll use the questions in a two-way conversation with God. Notice what you notice.

WORDS WITH GOD
OR
WORDS ABOUT GOD

I 've never played the game "Words with Friends" that has been so popular for the past few years, but I assume all three descriptors are important for the game to work: *words*, *with*, and *friends*. Words *about* friends are a whole different thing and it's not always a fun game in real life. Words *about* friends can lead to respect and influence when those words are genuine and uplifting. Other times, words *about* friends are actually an excuse for good old-fashioned gossip or hearsay that creates an invisible but palpable disconnect between people who never even got the chance to know one another or who only know *of* one another. I think words about God are similar.

Before we get into actual practices, I want to reiterate and explain a few things, especially about words with God and words about God.

This is not a theology book that is like most theological books I have read: words *about* God. The intention of this writing is not to persuade you into thinking a certain thing is correct or incorrect about God by convincing you that I am correct in my words or even in my experiences of God.

Here are my goals: I want to make hearing God an accessible practice for anyone who is interested regardless of their faith background. By *hearing* I mean *connection* and often that is beyond words. It involves visualizing, feeling, experiencing, and yes, also hearing words through language. So as I used the word *God*, please note that I'm using it for the purpose of playing this game: words with God, not just words about God.

I want anyone who reads this book to walk away with grounded, safe, and practical tools for living a two-way conversation with God.

Finally, my desire is to give you a powerful and easy guide that you can follow to practice freedom in your day-to-day life.

This means that I am most concerned about you engaging your words with God's words. A simple way to think of this is in the same vein that you would engage in a conversation with someone, directly. In the same room, talking to each other and listening to each other. The agenda is not important. Getting present, listening, and sharing is where the gold is found.

Words about God (theology) are not usually in the same territory as words with God (relational conversation and dialogue). But words with God will always give you words that you can use when you talk about God. Words about God don't always lead us to words with God. Words with God will always lead us to words about God. The order here is very important.

Much of my faith journey and the theology that I have studied in my lifetime has been, admittedly, a giant exercise of my ego.

I didn't realize it at the time, but for me, thinking about God played right into the deep pressure I experienced internally to figure out what was right and wrong in order to make sure I was always on the side of "right."

Come to find out, this is very human. Egoic pursuit is both fundamental and essential. But it always breaks down, and it is often not at all helpful, especially in pursuit of authentic connection.

Constantly on call, scanning the surface of our life for how to be right and avoid being in the wrong, takes its toll.

Needing to constantly check myself that I'm on the right side of right, whatever that has looked like for me and whatever that might have looked like for you—even if they look like polar opposites, is something that will forever be a shared human experience. As author and executive reinvention coach Tracy Goss explains, survival is the only game in town, and the paradigm of survival (needing to get it right and avoid being wrong) is the universal human paradigm. That means we all do a life dance that divides us.

So many times, I've pursued a knowledge of faith terms to make myself feel better about myself. I've labeled, categorized, judged, dismissed, violated, and hidden parts of myself, and I've silently endorsed, propped up, praised, and promoted other parts of me—this is the work of ego. But was any of that really "me?"

My version of the human paradigm has always included faith and God, which can get very sticky and confusing.

Am I actually experiencing God or my own egoic (get it right, avoid wrong) pursuit of a knowledge of God to serve my deep need for validation?

Who is God? Who are we? Why are we here? Who is my neighbor? How do I love my neighbors? What is salvation? Is there a hell? How do I get to heaven? How shall we live? What is the faith of Jesus and how do we put our faith in Jesus? What is the correct cultural interpretation of the Bible? Isn't the whole goal to align with right belief and faithful action? What is church?

Who is the Church? How are the best churches led? So many questions, ideas, and opinions.

These are really good questions and I imagine we as humans will be talking about things like this often and always.

But how will we continue to talk about them?

We could fight and draw lines around who believes what. Doesn't sound like much fun to me. I've done it enough.

We could simply argue and kindly point out what is wrong with each other's words about God. Not interested. I find this very boring and confining.

Or we could explore a land so vast and exciting because it's the territory of creation: what God is saying—God words. Hearing. Experiencing. Discovering. Sharing experiences. Learning. Practicing Enjoying.

The reality is that we won't always get it right. Even when we are committed to getting things right, we don't.

That's okay. When you practice talking with God, it requires the freedom to not have to get it right and the realistic understanding that we won't. But we're not showing up to get it right; we're showing up to know and to be known. To experience something far greater than the drive to survive, the pursuit of rules, the shoulds or should nots, the external validation we receive. or the internal insecurity we harbor.

Don't worry. We'll put practical parameters around hearing God to mitigate the risks.

I've found that sharing what I think I might be hearing from God with others who are doing the same helps a lot and becomes like a built-in safety net because God may use different words to talk to all of us, but the heart of it is the same.

Together, it's better. So before we dive into the "how-to's" of practice, an invitation:

I'm glad to share my own journey with you and what's helped me along the way. If it's helpful to you, run with it! I have pursued hearing God pretty much my entire life, but that doesn't mean it takes a lifetime to learn.

I'd be thrilled to hear about your journey and your experiences if you are interested in sharing find me on Curate. Our Mind Alchemy Curate App circle code is at the back of the book. This is for people who are interested in sharing words with God, with each other. It's not for God-word arguments or theological debate. There are other places for things like that. This group is for those interested in talking about a conversation with God for the joy of it, to learn, grow, and compare notes - it's a safe space to practice.

You can hear God now, today, easily. Jesus tells a parable about workers who show up at the end of the day to work the fields, and they get paid the same as those who showed up at the beginning of the day.

Showing up is the key. Timing is less important.

This is not a book about getting God right, but I acknowledge the very normal fear we as humans feel that often holds us back, not only from having a conversation with God but from honest conversations with ourselves and the people in our lives. It's vulnerable.

If you find yourself thinking, *But getting it right matters*, I completely understand. There is not a human alive who hasn't at some point in their life been entirely driven by the need to get it right (and therefore, the fear of getting it wrong). This is part and parcel of the human journey. It's just not possible, realistic, or actually all that important in the end.

If our pursuit is to get it right, we have already missed something very important: the entire point of theology—union, connection, sharing life, living fully, and all of life flourishing.

As a driver, our human addiction to being right and avoiding being wrong will always subvert our most authentic desires.

It will get in our way every single time whether we are aware of it or not.

Needing to be right is not actually the way of life. It turns out to be the way of self-sabotage, because even at its best, it requires self-judgment and self-division. These self-inflicted pain points will always spill over to inflicting others with them because that's how life works—osmosis is a thing.

One of my favorite moments in the life of Jesus is when we see Him pray a heartfelt prayer before he is handed over to the Roman government to be killed. His conversation with God reveals His heart's motivation for us: that we would be one. Undivided. Right vs. wrong. Even using good discourse and right thinking about God will always leave us segmented. Words about God will cease but words with God can be enjoyed in every language, forever. Tuning in will be our very practical and essential practice.

Original Connection

Why can any human hear God? Original connection. Before the origin story of sin (the broken experiences that come out of this lie: we are lacking), is the original story of great interconnection.

The original story from Genesis 1 and 2 about what it is to be a human made in the image of God is an incredible glimpse at the human journey.

Humans were made well, lacking nothing. "Very good" by God's very words. The walking, breathing, talking embodiment of God's own love, life, and breath in human flesh.

The glory of a glorious creation. A chip off the old block. Nothing hidden. No shame. Born into a beautiful world to explore.

And yet, as the story goes, it is the human experience to have everything and think that we are missing something.

This is what plays out in the Garden of Paradise: Adam and Eve had everything they needed and wanted. But somehow they didn't know it. Somewhere in there, they thought they were lacking something. The offer to become more like God and see is not something they would have desired if they had known that they already were like God and they already had full access to God's viewpoint. The temptation ultimately: reject who you are as a child of God and become God. The lie: being a human made in the image of God and being with God was not enough. This is the same lie the ego feeds on to pursue Godlikeness. Not enough. Wrong. Missing something. Lacking. Not yet right. Must do more, be more, accomplish more, and then we won't lack. The problem was never that we weren't perfect or "there yet" is the idea that we're lacking. More and better doesn't dissipate the fear that we are lacking.

The fruit of the tree of the knowledge of good and evil is a metaphor for the human formation journey. Born into a loving connection with our Creator, we still end up

looking for what? For something *more* right than being present with God. This has always led to a burden, judgment, division, and death of the real dream: union and presence. The most common way we experience this death is with a low level, under-the-surface dissatisfaction, and disconnection. Taken to its extreme, we feel like a fraud and then we begin to act like one.

The great human fear of being wrong or not enough, whatever that looks like for you, is what people in our lifetime have come to describe as the ego—the false self. Adam and Eve ate from the ego tree to know about God, themselves, and the world apart from the living words of God. Know about good, what's right, know about evil, how to avoid being wrong, and now I am powerful, like God. Except I feel ill-equipped to maintain this level of judgment because I'm a human designed for living, not a God able to know the end from the beginning.

The problem here, and I'd argue it's not really that much of a problem but part of the maturity process, is that the pursuit of the fruit came from immature self-knowledge. Eve and Adam already had the thing they were seeking: to be like God. They were. Part and parcel, made in the image of God. They already lived in the garden. They already walked with God. They had access, provision, protection, empowerment, and family. Perhaps what they needed was the discovery of what is. "What is" was in place and wonderful, but the discovery and awakening to "what is" is a good and beautiful human journey.

The problem is not dysfunction. The issue is misunderstood or an under-valued connection. The tree of life satisfies our built-in capacity for union and connection. The tree of knowing good and evil reinforces that which only connection to life will satisfy.

The false self cannot navigate its way to the Tree of Life because the false self was created from a perceived lack. When the lack is no longer perceived, the false self is like the mist or cloud of vapor that has passed from view and from the mind.

Notice that I didn't use the phrase "the bad self," that's not it. The reason I use the word "false" as many have before me, is that when we as humans need to be right and must avoid being wrong, we are living from a lie that is false but not *bad*; it arose from what was really good—a free will and a desire to learn and grow.

When we live driven by the unconscious ulterior motive of proving something wrong or right, we consistently betray who we are. We do this because we are not conscious of what is real about our being.

What is real? Genesis 1. I'm not arguing that we were created in seven days. I'm interested in what the poetic story tells us about our relationship with God, self, and the world around us. We are a very good creation: humans made by love in the image of God, filled by the breath of God, and this is an on-purpose expression of the beauty and goodness of God.

Awareness of this underlying, forever truth will always mean that we have nothing to prove. Our rightness is a state of existence, not something to prove but to discover. Fear about being wrong melts when we realize we are loved, known, and connected to God as humans. It's not a mistake that we exist as humans, and it's never been a requirement that we become like God; that's been accounted for in our design.

When we are obsessed with a knowledge of good or a knowledge of evil and we must be right to feel okay about ourselves, we will continue to self-validate and self-flagellate by eating more from the tree that tells us there's something more we're missing! It will never be enough.

The fruit of the tree that brings death offers us a severe trade-off: experience everything, even your relationship with God and self, through the lens of right and wrong, judging what is good and evil, like God. What did we trade? God was trying to spare us from the burden of actually being God—children of God, yes. God, no. It's not a task human beings are made for, and it will continue to crush us as long as we think we must become Godlike. Our only salvation is to realize we already are. Already loved. Already connected. Already "in" the family. Already enough, just right, very good. We are a chip off the old block. Jesus says he came to show us that we are actually already one with His Father. He came to show us what is real, not how to make up for what we deem we lack.

We are who we are: children of God, created by God. You cannot uncreate yourself. Find me the person who wasn't made by the hands of a good and loving Father, birthed from the womb of the always creating Mother, filled with the very spirit—in Hebrew, ruah, or breath—of the ever-present Immanuel God.

Where can you, created one, go from God's presence? To hell? No, not even there can you find refuge from God's never-ending love. To Egypt? God's there. If you found your way to the very depth of the sea, you would find that you are surrounded forever by the love of the God who made you. It's in you. It is you.

When I say this book is not about theology as you know it, I mean that even if you don't "believe" anything I just wrote. It doesn't matter. Let me explain.

If we were on a beach trip and you slept until 10:00 a.m. in a room with blackout curtains and I came to wake you saying, "The sun's up, let's go for a walk!" but you didn't believe me. You might respond with, "It's the middle of the night. I'm going back to sleep." I may open a curtain or I might just let you sleep, but it doesn't change the fact that the sun is shining on our plot of land brightly at that moment, 10:00 a.m.

Theology has been presented often as a correct thought about God, or for our example, knowing that the sun is out. Do you believe the sun is out and that it is 10:00 a.m., which may or not be correct? Is the sun shining now or not? Is the time correctly described, or is it just an hour we all agreed to call 10:00 a.m? It doesn't actually matter. What matters is that I want to talk and walk with my friend. My friend wants to sleep and both desires are valid. How will we respond to one another in love?

In the next section, we'll think (use our thoughts, minds, emotions, and rememberings) to have a conversation with ourselves and with God. We'll learn to think with God as a practice and practical experience instead of thinking about God as if we were separated and living in a vacuum far from God.

It will be intellectual, but not for the purpose of being right intellectually about God. Experiencing a connection with God is always beautiful and intellectual, meaning it makes good use of the intellect.

Let Section 2 two be a personal practice guide for you whether you think the sun is out or not.

It's for you whether you use the name Jesus or Yeshua or, "Hey, God, are you even real?" when you engage in a conversation with God. The honest way is the only way, and that is something only you can choose.

Let's take a walk on the beach and we'll experience whatever hour it is together. You don't even have to call it a beach to walk on it. You can call it a turf. You can call it the beautiful oceanside. You could call it no man's land or never, never land. You could even go walk on this beach with me and call the beach under your feet your imagination. That's fine. Let's just take the walk.

If you find your ego protesting, thank it for wanting to keep you safe and acknowledge all you have learned in your pursuit of being right. Then take a look at what you really want. Is the authentic heartbeat inside of you deeply desiring to be right? I doubt it. Beyond the realm of getting things right is the realm of desire. God-given hunger. The ego wonders if it's wrong and likely has judged your desires as selfish and off-limits at some point in your life, but there they are, and they remain. I'm not talking about false desires for image-centric things or things that harm you. That's not what you actually want. The real question is one I learned from my friend and brilliant re-invention coach Tracy Goss. She calls it "the Spice Girls question." Yep. Tell me what you want, what you really really want.

Why did you pick up this book? What do you want, really? I doubt it's to be right about hearing God, even if that's an understandable and rational thought you've had. If you didn't have to worry about that concern, what do you actually want?

I'm guessing we're not too different. I really want an authentic connection. If there is a real, accessible experience of God, I want to enjoy it. I want to hear God for real. I want wisdom. I want to be present in the beauty that is my life. I don't want to be numb. I really do have questions for God that I want to explore and hear the answer that is real straight from the Source. I've heard from others. I am interested in what God describes to Moses as face-to-face. In the story of Moses when God speaks on Mount Sinai there's this moment where God tells Moses to bring everyone there to hear for themselves face-to-face together. Moses tells everyone, "It's time to go talk to God!" But the people are scared for their lives. They say, *you* go and you tell us what God says, Moses. I may have done the same thing if I had been there. I have functionally, in my formative years, very much wanted other people especially leader type "Moseses" to tell me what God says. What did God say, pastor? What does it mean?

Don't we all find ourselves in the life of Moses? At times, bad with words. Uncertain. Passionate one minute and fleeing the next. We too, just like

Moses, have been invited into a relationship of face-to-face communication and presence.

We all want to be invited, but do we know that we are? We have been from day one. We were made to connect through communication. Your thought life is fertile ground for communication with God because it was designed to be the central communication platform for your life. I wonder how many Israelites died in that desert within months of an invitation to see and hear God face-to-face? They were afraid they'd die, held back and stuck with what they knew, and died anyway.

SECTION TWO

Chapter 1—

THE THREAT OF EMBODIMENT

"And God said, 'Let there be light,' and there was light. God saw that the light was good, and separated the light from the darkness. God called the light 'day,' and called the darkness 'night.'" And there was evening, and there was morning—the first day."

"In the beginning was the Word, and the Word was with God, and the Word was God. He was with God in the beginning. Through him all things were made; without him nothing was made that has been made. In him was life, and that life was the light of all (hu)mankind."[2]

Who you really are is what threatens you most. Nothing else could sustain *that* kind of power over you. The threat remains because of the reality of your existence that you must own to move past the threat. An unowned life is a threatened existence. Why? Because you are literally from light, you are made of light and nothing less than being the light that you are will satisfy the elements that comprise your being.

What threatens us as humans the most is not what we think it is. It isn't lack, fear, shame, isolation, failure, or rejection. Those are normal and common

---

2.   John 1:1–4 (NIV).

to every human. We'll look at them in the coming chapters but they aren't the real threat, not really. What threatens us the most is stepping outside of these human experiences (at times, havens) into a full embrace of who we were born to be—it has nothing to do with a voice other than your own. Lack can't speak to it. Shame can't distort it. Fear will not outlast it. Who you really, *really are,* the part of you that was baked into the fabric of your existence, is inescapably good, smart, free, important, and powerful. Quite threatening indeed.

That person, subconsciously, is your biggest threat. That person is who you resist, belittle, and evade for fear that she or he is some version of bad, wrong, off, broken, tainted, or simply not quite enough. Understanding how mind alchemy works begins with understanding that your only sure move in life is to deeply embrace who God made you to be—who you already *are.* I guarantee you this has been your number one struggle in life. At the very least, it has been significantly challenged.

Here's the good news, we can easily find and dismantle your number one struggle (there really is no other) if we can uncover the real you. Now you know. Now you can focus. Basic human survival instinct points to this reality: you were born to discover the beautiful existence that you are, therefore you must survive. But survival mode will keep you fighting other threats, avoiding the real one: you.

Our instinct to survive knows something your everyday cognitive brain may not: despite being threatened by all that you are and all you will become, *you're* worth saving. You are worth fighting for.

What if our survival instinct was more than primordial? What if it's screaming something few have heard: your life is worth living?

The struggle is real for good reason. Who you are is not easily pin-downable. Identity is always a discovery—even for the most well-identified in the world (think about for example a British monarch—born a king, yet the discovery of what that identity really is takes a lifetime). The only journey you are really on is the journey of discovery.

On the first day of creation, God says this simple sentence, "Let there be light." And it was. And you are. We are. The whole world is made up of an incredible spectrum of light, most of which we cannot see with our natural eyes. Every spot you see in the night sky that is a beautiful hue of midnight black and blue is as light and bright as the brightest star. It's 100 percent light. Our eyes only read a very small portion of the light waves that exist, weaving all of creation into a connected symphony of light. Did you know that light exists as both a particle and a wave? That's why what you are about to practice will work whether you understand it or not.

Practice 1: Light

Close your eyes. (After you read this short paragraph.)
Notice the light. That's right, eyes wide shut. Describe what you notice about the quality of light. Take a few moments to just feel the light that exists even as you rest your eyes.

Now slowly open them and keep noticing what you notice. Notice how the quality of light changes as you open your eyelids. What light is your eye drawn to? Write a description of what you notice now.

This is the basic first movement of transforming anything you are thinking, especially in the realm of self-expression, from a normal, basic, or negative thought into something literally laced with golden light in your mind.

Now that you've noticed the light in general with your eyes shut and open, let's practice with a thought. Think about something in your life that could use a little light. It might be a situation going on in your life or something just rolling around in your thoughts. Notice how it comes to mind. Does it come as a scenario? Does it come with dread about the past or future? Does it come in the form of a little movie or picture in your mind? Does it come with a sense of insignificance or a feeling of "this isn't that important, I don't know why it came to mind?" Anything goes. Just notice what and how it comes. What feelings are connected to it? Just take note and be honest with yourself—good, bad, and ugly. Don't judge it, just notice, describe it, and now, **picture it in the light.**

Notice what happens as light is exposed to it or as you notice *where the light is* **around that thought.** Notice the interplay of light and the scenario of your thoughts. The light, as you notice it in your mind, may appear in another area. That's fine, just notice what you notice. What questions does it bring up for you?

Three easy steps and all they require is honest noticing:

1. Note any situation/thought.

2. Notice the light.

3. Notice what questions surface. Ask yourself what you are curious about now?

Situation/Thought:

Notice the Light:

What questions come to mind? What are you curious about now?

What happened for you as you practiced noticing the light? Describe how your heart, mind, and body feel now.

As you practice noticing the light, it may seem unimportant (whatever you happened to be noticing) because it can be boiled down to a few words and phrases about what you see as normal life scenarios. It's not unimportant; it's where you are now, and it's real to you. So be present to it without jumping in to judge whether it is or isn't of importance.

Understanding who "you" are is a process and could never be encapsulated in one word, experience, or phrase. You will have many words, experiences, memories, and creative ideas that rise from who you are and resonate with who you are, but one word will never do it justice. One phrase or one experience or one memory could never fully capture it. And yet we must use words and phrases at all different stages of life to describe what we are experiencing and discovering to be true. Do not be detoured simply because you are still mid-discovery. Do not be dismayed because you feel as though you simply don't know and haven't arrived. Those things are true and will always be true. There will be much you don't know and you will never arrive. At the same time, there's much you do know and you are here now. You have arrived where you are. Can you value that?

Don't let seemingly mundane processes of discovery in life deceive you into thinking you are not on a path that is vibrant and congruent with who you are. You are mid-discovery and you cannot escape who and what you are. This is *good* news. The more you slow down, notice, and appreciate your life and how you think about it, the quicker you will find that there is a path and you are on it.

The seven practices are laser focused on creating a very specific space for you. The "you" who you were created to be, who you really are will emerge freely in this space. You are not the sum total of your thoughts, but your thoughts will impact how you think, feel, and perceive yourself. *Think of your thoughts less as defining and more as communications to process.* For example, if you have a greedy thought, you are not greedy. If you have a shame-filled thought, it doesn't mean you "are" shame. You might have a suicidal thought, but it doesn't mean you are suicidal. In the same vein, you might have a brilliant idea, but you aren't the idea. You might have a kind thought, but it doesn't mean you are kind. It's what you choose to embody about your thoughts (what do you enact?) that you become. And is what you choose to embody what you actually want to embody? Is it congruent with the light that you are? Maybe so, maybe not. The only way to learn to discern the difference is to start noticing your thoughts. That's why every practice is grounded in thinking about the way you think—noticing.

The practices are generative by design, in order on purpose, and declarative.

Let's look at that:

1. Generative by design.

2. In order on purpose.

3. Declarative.

Generative by design: They create simply by the way they are designed. They are creative in nature. Notice, I didn't say that they are constructive, meaning putting something together piece by piece. Instead, I am focusing on these two words when I say generative: they are *creative (they create) and reproductive (life-giving)*. Anything that is generative fundamentally functions with the ability to produce and reproduce. Merriam-Webster gives these synonyms for the word generative:

*   Producing
*   Yielding

- Bearing
- Cornucopian
- Fertile
- Fruitful
- Lush
- Luxuriant
- Productive
- Prolific
- Rich
- Abundant
- Copious
- Generous
- Bountiful
- Liberal
- Plentiful
- Blooming
- Bursting
- Flourishing
- Swarming
- Teeming
- Thriving
- Creative
- Inventive
- Original

Here are the antonyms, what generative is not:

- Barren
- Dead
- Infertile
- Sterile

- Unfertile
- Unfruitful
- Unproductive
- Meager
- Scant
- Skimpy
- Spare
- Sparse

Generative by design means these practices have a very important thing built into them: they will not leave you lacking.

In order on purpose: they are created to flow together. You can focus on one as we have in this first chapter of Section 2—Light. You could spend a day, a week, a season, or a year doing a deep dive into just one, but they were created in an order on such purpose that you will find one draws you into the other. As you practice one (light), it will flow into two (God's kind of division) so naturally that you may have already crept into practice two without realizing it in the simple practice we just did.

The practices are in order, on purpose, and you'll find the ordered flow to be both helpful and it will bring a sense of completion to you as you keep practicing.

Declarative: Oxford Languages online says the word "declarative" can be used as an adjective to describe this action:

- Of the nature of or making a declaration.

- Denoting high-level programming languages which can be used to solve problems without requiring the programmer to specify an exact procedure to be followed.

Or declarative can be used as a noun:

- A statement in the form of a declaration.

The word declaration comes from a Latin word meaning to "make quite clear." And the dictionary says a declaration is a "formal announcement of the beginning of a state or condition." While much action will arise and can arise from these practices, on their most basic level they are declarations that, as the definition says, do not require you to specify an exact procedure to be followed.

This can be confusing at first because you will not always need an action plan. Your action plan is first and foremost declaration-based. Where do we first see declarations that create comprehensive specificity without being declaratively specific? Genesis 1. The *let there be's*. God uses "Let there be" declarations to create the entire universe.

If your life was created through generative declarations, what do you think could happen if you aligned your thoughts and words with the same declarations that gave birth to you? You will become who you are, whoever that is, free from the limits of thoughts that are old, stuck, or something other than your own.

Do not worry, it's not rocket science to practice; it's far more simple. Simple does not mean uncomplex, dumb, or easy. It does mean it's brilliantly designed for access.

This book is really about access. These practices will give you *access* to who you are and how to be it. Maybe better said, how to free and unleash it.

Chapter 2–

THE THREAT OF DEVELOPMENT

There is a healthy kind of separation. It's not the kind that draws lines between things and calls one side good and the other bad. The kind of division that we see on Day Two of creation is a model for the power of boundaries. Lines of distinction allow for the ocean and the sky to exist in interdependent harmony and beauty. The boundary between the pond and the mudbank encompassing it allows the birds to find their water and provides a solid piece of earth for them to rest on as well. But the boundary we see is much less of a line and far more of a space where two systems become one. The water seeps into the soil. The soil seeps into the water. The two very different elements mingle, literally becoming blurred lines that create a whole new expression of connection. From afar, it looks like there's a distinct dividing line between the pond and the land. Up close, on a cellular level, there is oneness, the healthiest kind of blurred line. There are valuable distinctions built into life that help us to see the beauty of the world around us. They teach us by offering us the chance to understand nuances and differences.

Negative space is good art.

Find me an acclaimed artist who doesn't honor or use negative space masterfully. They do not exist because one way or another, art requires masterful use of what is called "negative space" in design. Sara Barnes wrote a piece for My Modern Met about negative space. She explains it this way:

> So don't underestimate negative space. Just because it might be bare doesn't mean that it lacks power. By removing elements of an image, it can evoke mystery and conjure emotions of longing or loss. When used in this way, negative space helps drive the larger meaning behind a work.[3]

Look at the space that isn't filled, or doesn't at first glance seem to be filled with anything in your favorite works of art; this is what is referred to as negative space. Look at the shapes that arise from the space between. If a true-to-life drawing is rendered, there is no way to distinguish anything without negative space. No rest for the eyes.

The demarcation line between objects doesn't create a disconnect. It actually creates a border that allows us to understand how everything is connected. The cohesion and connection in a piece of art are augmented by spacial definition, not threatened by it.

There is a kind of separation and boundary that creates beauty and definition. Distinctions and divisions are meant to cause life to thrive, connection to exist, and value to be derived. The kind of distinction lines God creates cause a healthy interdependence, not a codependence or the kind of division that sets one apart violently. When we as humans judgmentally devalue through the misuse of distinction, violence is birthed. What will boundaries and distinctions produce in your mind? What is being produced for you? Honor or judgment? Freedom or fear? If boundaries and distinctions do not stir up

---

3.   Sara Barnes, "How Artists Use Negative Space to Say a Lot with Nothing," My Modern Met, June 21, 2019, https://mymodernmet.com/negative-space-definition/.

curiosity that brings growth, healing, connection, and freedom to you and others, it's likely a false version of boundaries.

When subtle voices of fear, shame, and insecurity speak to us about distinctions, they make our world very small and reduce our understanding of reality into something that is, yes, seemingly simple but completely inaccurate and delusional. Everything must now fit into the made-up categories of good or bad. Wrong or right. Healthy or unhealthy. True or untrue. Crazy or sane. We trade the color lenses that were created for us on day one of creation—where everything is literally made up of light and teeming with life, a spectrum of intense beauty in all its shades and hues for a nuance-less black and white lie.

Do the boundaries in your life create life for you and others or do they violate it?

Just writing about this stirs up so many thoughts for me. What about you? Can you feel in your body as you notice it, the difference between distinction lines that bring more life and connection and division lines that separate us from real life? Do you know the difference I'm referring to? Can you think of boundaries that have brought more life to your own and others, and can you see how even holding on to what may have been a "healthy" boundary past its expiration date can cause it to function like a prison?

When I was a kid, my mom told me never to cross the street alone. If I still held this as an essential truth for me, I'd literally be stuck quite often in my life—the healthy childhood boundary now limiting my movement in the world.

Our own development (aka change) will often appear at first to our naked human experience as a threat. This is normal and understandable. Do you sense it? The coming changes that might threaten your status quo, your immature edges? It's normal to be threatened, but you can flip the switch on this one and see it for the gift it is: you're made to handle big changes and development. It's for you and though it seems that it will break you, it will actually *make* you.

Let's take a breath here. Literally, that's the most basic form of Practice 2.

Practice 2: God's Kind of Separation

God's kind of separation is happening all the time. It functions very well and it's for us. The easiest way to find this natural occurrence happening is in your breath.

1. Breathe in (note the life-giving substance released by the plants and trees around you now filling your lungs, calming your nerves, and allowing you to live your life for another minute).

2. Breathe out (note the exhalation of what could be a toxic substance if trapped in your lungs but what turns out to be just what the plants around you find useful to keep going and growing).

3. Deepen your inhale. Breathe in through your nose and let it fill your lower stomach cavity first, then your lower chest, and, last, your upper chest. Fill the front of your body *and* equally, the back of your body, bottom to top. Hold it till you need to let it go and…

4. Slowly exhale. Take your time. Pause and repeat. In. Pause. Out. Pause. Take your time (just one to two minutes is all you need). Notice what you notice:

As you breathe, what do you notice about your body? (It can be anything!)

What does your body feel as you start breathing?

What does your body feel after one minute of deeper breathing?

What do you notice about your mind as you start to breathe?

Notice what comes across the screen of your mind as you breathe.

When you are done, check in with your mind. How does it feel now?

Check in with your heart, your emotions, and desires. What do you feel?

What are you curious about right now?

Notice what you notice…

Remember the thought you brought into your mind with the light. Remember what you noticed? Now let's notice what happens when we simply declare, (in your mind or out loud) "Let there be God's kind of separation." Then just notice what you "see" on the communication screen of your mind. Notice what you notice. Is there a type of distinction coming to mind that is helpful for you? Is there a question coming to mind? If so, ask the question on the screen of your mind. Go ahead and make it a real declarative question by either writing it out, thinking it clearly in your mind, or saying it out loud. Now note what comes to mind right after you ask the question:

_____

_____

_____

_____

_____

_____

Your body is a network of systems where definition and distinct boundaries are essential for it all to work together to allow you to read this book now. You are a living and breathing artwork full of defining lines, like the boundaries of a river, causing your blood to flow fast and freely enabling everything about your movement in the world.

You are defined and distinguished by the intricate separations designed by your Source to give you life. While this is real and true, probably because it IS real and true, it can function also as a real threat to us.

While there is certainly a type of separation we can employ via judgment that divides humanity in the most destructive ways, there's also a healthy form of separation that takes place during development and growth that we resist and fear because it requires change, both internally and externally. The threat doesn't show up well for us. It doesn't knock on our door and explain: I'm here to grow you and develop you into a greater version of yourself. Instead, it often arrives unannounced and is laden with challenges. It can show up as our worst fear coming true, the unexpected arriving when we least expected it, or it can present as breakdown, failure, depression, or a mixture of them all.

It can create pressure that moves us into the very unhelpful realm of distinction: the comparative realm. It threatens us by pointing out all of our differences and offering fear as a solution. Misunderstanding and condemnation is its middle name but it won't tell you that. Instead, it adopts surnames like certainty or conviction. As an uninvited visitor to your life, development can create a narrative that tells me not only that I'm different and bad, but that maybe you are different and bad and we are not in the same boat, much less in the same family.

The perceived threat of development and growth can cause such anxiety if we are unaware of what is happening, that it creates separations that are not real. They are illusions of separation and the false perception yields little but pain and torment.

While the real distinctions and separations of life continue to creatively define us and grow us, we can lose sight of these altogether if we are threatened by the very thing that wants to give us what we want: growth and development.

Getting unstuck and out of the false narrative is easy when you can see it and notice how it feels to be in it.

"Let there be God's kind of separation!"

There's another way to say it. Take any thought, whether you deem it small or large, important or unimportant, or in between; it really doesn't matter. Just pick one.

Now think, say, or write this: There is God's kind of separation. Now watch. By watch I mean notice your thought formations as soon as you say this. What do you notice? What changes? What doesn't? What images enter your mind? What words? What feelings? You may only notice one small change and it might only be perceived by how you feel or your intuition. Notice it and see what it produces. What do I mean by "see what it produces?" I mean notice what you notice about what you notice. Is it helpful? Fruitful? Stabilizing? Does it seem to come from a clarifying place and create clarity? Does it confuse you? What next best question does it lead you to? Formulate that, and then ask it. Here's a table to help you track what we just did.

Pick a thought, any thought.

Say, write, or think: "There is God's kind of separation."

Notice what you notice. Ask the next best question and record again what you notice after asking.

On day two of creation God speaks about a separation that created one of my favorite things about life on earth: the beauty of the ocean and the sky. Think about a sunset over the ocean and all the interactions that are crossing the lines of what your eye reads as a boundary. The sun refracting and reflecting across sky, waves, and seashore. The water evaporating into the sky and sinking into the sand again and again with each rush of the current. Beauty requires life-giving symbiotic boundaries but it doesn't stop the connection, interdependence, and new formation.

Life-giving separation creates the spaces we hold most dear. Like negative space in a great piece of art, the dividing lines reveal. They comfort. They clarify. They fill. They allow us to be still. They delight and surprise.

Like a wave returning to the ocean, the negative space of life is where the seashells are discovered. The negative spaces of your life create a new landscape, if only for moments. The negative space is not to be avoided but it's an invitation to live life in harmony with the preexisting rhythms of life. Connected yet distinct. Outlined but shared lines. Without the space between, there's no rhythm, no music, no heartbeat, no life.

You, the master artist of your life, will discover the beauty of the masterpiece that *is* your life when you are willing to embrace the negative space. Ignoring it will never work. Evading it is impossible. Trying to rid your life of it will leave you feeling and looking like a kid with finger paints who has mixed them all up and created a big swampy colored blob on his paper. His masterpiece reflects freedom and creative power, but it will never truly reflect the nuances of life until someone teaches him about lines, negative space, and perspective. You are a distinct and unique creation that is uniquely and distinctly unified and connected to life both through the light that you are and the lines that cause you to appear distinctly as yourself in the world.

When we are threatened by our own distinctions and others'—when we are obsessed with sameness, we end up in the mire of judgment which will always bring about the kind of separation that kills us. When we can notice and value distinction, our own and others', we find that in our uniqueness, we will always be unified. Not the same, but connected as one. The sea and the sky are not the same, but they function uniquely as one.

Negative space is good art, so it comes as no surprise to me that it's God's second move in declaring the "let it be's" of life.

For forty-one years I have read and heard the Genesis story. For thirty-eight years of hearing it, I never saw the beauty and power of the kind of separation that God does. It's the wisdom of the Creator to distinguish. It's the pain of indistinguished people to divide in a way that derides. The division is natural to life, derision is not. The rest of the flow of creation will affirm the life-giving nature of creative separation. This is not segregation. It's flow. God separates the waters.

What waters you? Think about "the waters" that flow into your mind. All kinds of things flow in and out.

The creative statement, "Let there be a separation of the waters" is a statement of release. Let the waters flow and separate according to the creativity of God for the purpose and function of free and creative flow.

God knows I need this every day. The waters roll in but which are for me today? Which will nourish and direct me? Which are beneficial to my life? Which are worth drinking from and which are better left to be swept out to sea with today's current? Am I threatened by the intimidating life force known as growth? It's normal, so breathe through it and be brave. Look again and see what it's doing to create beauty and distinction in your life.

There is an ebb and flow between the interior landscape of self we have been gifted with and called to by God—the body and soul and spirit made in the image of God and sustained by God's very breath—and the landscape of the world around us. The very ground we stand on is a terrain we are intricately connected to but also one that seems foreign and not the same as what's inside of you. One "territory" you have been given to fully occupy, another to inhabit—to bless, fill, and multiply within. If you can practice the ebb/flow of alternating awareness—in out, then out in, then in and out again—you will learn naturally about healthy boundaries. You will notice where you begin and others end as far as an occupation goes (this is limited to the self) and you'll recognize that where you end is actually where you and all else begin beyond you. You will value the transition and the space of interconnectedness or symbiosis.

Your ebb and flow is threefold: body, emotion, and breath. Take a moment to scan these three very personal "territories" and notice where you sense God, where you sense yourself, and where you sense others. In the twenty-one day Out of Box Appendix on Day 12, there's a very simple tool that I use every day multiple times a day that helps me do this.

Chapter 3—

THE THREAT OF DISCOVERY

I lived in a cage of anxiety as a kid. I was often nervous to the point of a stomach ache but it was particularly worse anytime I was in a new environment. The first day of school every year was the worst. Avoiding eye contact as much as possible, I entered my new classroom with the goal of drawing zero attention to myself so that my heart could stop racing and I could position myself quickly behind the shelter of the cold iron desk-chair combo ideally at the back of the room—a much safer position than walking, talking or interacting with people. I remember the almost constant feeling of anxiety that I carried, but I also distinctly remember that I had no idea where it came from. Discovery? Absolute threat because I felt so nervous about exposure. Be discovered by others? No, thank you. Discover things on my own, maybe if I had nothing else to do. Discover things freely through learning at school? Also a no for me. That would require me to let myself go at school—too dangerous to be seen, to feel uncovered. I felt the "dis" in covered as a threat that I was not willing to endure. I resisted the greatness of discovery because of severe anxiety.

Shame is not the word I would have used for it at the time. All I knew was that I felt it. A familiar frenemy. It kept me safe-ish. It also kept me boxed in and busy keeping all my fears at bay.

Kindergarten's first day I've completely blocked out, since it must have been a fear-fest. First grade I can remember vividly because I was in a new school, I knew no one, and I naturally assumed everyone else was the best of friends already. Second grade was not any better on the anxiety and shame front, but then when third grade rolled around, everything changed.

On this particular first day, the unexpected happened. All my worst fears about what could happen on the first day of school did not happen. (Fear narrative: I get lost and cause a scene trying to find my class, I have to raise my hand and speak out loud for more than a one-word answer, I have something on me that's disgusting and I don't know about it, I trip on my way to the pencil sharpener, I'm seen or worse, given attention by everyone.) On the first day of third grade, I walked into Mrs. Christianson's class. I had no idea at the time that she would become my favorite teacher, and I had no way of knowing that the sweet girl sitting to my right would become a lifelong friend. The new girl's name was Stacy Dollar.

I noticed her immediately, and I imagine everyone else did too. Not only was she new but she was beautiful, notably beautiful. Not only was she *beautiful* but she was half Apache and to a group of third graders, that fact alone made her semi-famous. Her dad gave talks on being a full-blooded American Indian and growing up at Cal Farley's Boys Ranch as a young child. He tells about how he met Jesus and how it changed everything about his life. He found in Jesus a home, a purpose, and a new life. Not only is his story genuinely amazing, but at a small Christian school, with an audience of third graders, it plays really well. Especially when he shows up dressed like his ancestors and sings story songs. I'm getting ahead of myself here but third-grade kids can just sense the cool factor when it comes to things like this, so even though we didn't yet know about Soapy Dollar, we knew Stacy was special.

I hate to admit how much she made me feel better because it's pretty cheap but it's completely true. (Stace, I don't think I ever told you this!) When the teacher called the roll for the very first time on the very first day, as nervous as I was that my name would be read wrong again, and I'd have to correct her out loud in front of everyone, what Stacy did before we got to my name shocked my nerves into a state of calm.

"Stacy Dollar?" Mrs. Christianson read aloud. Silence. I noticed that Stacy was trying to covertly wave to the teacher without being seen and without having to say a word. I knew immediately what she was doing. Her epidermis (do you remember when kids would use that joke incessantly?) was showing, as was mine. She did not want to be seen but there she was, in the flesh, in a moment that demanded a response.

"Stacy, are you okay?" our patient teacher asked. Stace wasn't gonna do it. She was refusing to do the thing that I, too, certainly didn't want to do: speak up.

She was so against opening her mouth publicly that she took the risk of a walk to the front of the classroom (bold!) over saying something out loud.

Finally, I was watching a beautiful, seemingly capable and confident girl who looked from outside appearances to be fun, friendly, and clearly her own brand of special, act even more afraid of people than I felt.

And this is the part I feel a pang of self-judgment admitting. Watching Stacy struggle, I felt better. So. Much. Better. I didn't even wince when the teacher said my name wrong. "I'm here, and it's CaycE."

Later I found out that Stacy really needed to use the bathroom but was far too embarrassed to ask for that at the start of day one, so she approached the bench to whisper her request. I get it, for those of us with childhood social anxiety, we totally get that move and why she made it. Not only do I have respect for what Stacy did that day, but I remember it *this* vividly because, for some reason, it broke an invisible box open for me.

I didn't even know how desperate I was to get out of that box.

That box wasn't actually rational or helpful to me beyond a certain feeling of personal comfort, but that's the thing about human boxes—they don't actually fit or flow with what's naturally rational or helpful to us. Boxes seem rational when we are in them, because by their nature they are habitable and for that, we feel some gratitude. But that gratitude only lasts so long. Eventually, we feel like we are stuck in a musty box in the dark when we're in them, because we are. We can't see ourselves, we can't move well, and we can't relate with anyone else in an authentic way. It was easy jumping into the box, but the truth is that life in the box is surprisingly complicated by the simple parameters of the box. Discovery in a box only happens in one lane: the discovery that the box is not where you want to be. See how the things that truly threaten us are always there lurking behind the scenes trying to help us *out*?

As a quick look at how life in a box functions, let's use my third-grade box as an example.

We could call that particular box many things but for our purposes here let's call it the "I'm terrified of everything, especially attention at school" box.

The "I'm terrified of everything, especially attention at school" box came with some clear parameters. Here are what the four walls of this box said to me.

First, the most basic of walls: the shoulds and should nots:

- I shouldn't say a word, then I might be embarrassed.
- I shouldn't draw attention to myself.

- I should look right, think right, know how to do everything correctly, and if I must speak, say the right things.
- I should hide behind anything and anyone else.
- I shouldn't be seen or show myself (low-key personality).
- I shouldn't mess anything up or come across as bad/wrong.
- I should be good but not so good that I get too much attention for it.

Next, the box brought a set of "oughts or ought nots." An ought is generally a bit stronger and deeper than a should, more of a code or vow than a general directive thought.

- I ought to be someone else.
- I ought to be quiet.
- I ought to be good.
- I ought not cause a commotion.
- I ought to be very easy.
- I ought not be silly or disrespectful.
- I ought not move (I told you they aren't entirely rational on the surface).

Then, as all interpersonal boxes do, the box offered strong and clear "Must always or could nevers":

- I must always comply.
- I must never be the center of attention.
- I must always hold back my thoughts/ideas/real self.
- I must always defer.
- I must never be flashy or loud.
- I must fear in order to not be unsafe.

Finally, there's the wall with some holes poked in it, the "I would if I could" or "If I could, I would" wall:

- If I could, I would stop worrying all the time.
- If I could, I would have fun.
- If I could, I would enjoy playing.
- If I could, I would relax.
- If I could, I would discover all the things I'm curious about and like the most!

Looking back on these shoulds, oughts, musts, and woulds—from the perspective of thirty more years of maturity and life experience, none of these statements feel accurate or real. But I remember, as a nine year old, that they were my world. I lived by them.

Watching Stacy jolted me out of my comfort with the very confining box that was dominating my personal narrative and actions.

At the time, I had no idea what a box was or that I was in one. I was surviving and doing the best I could. Just like you did when you were in third grade and just like we're all doing now. Over the next three decades, that residue of shame and anxiety would drive me to seek a much broader understanding of what freedom is available, what healing I needed, and most importantly, what is it to be a human?

This chapter and Day 3 is for anyone who is feeling the confines of a box—Day 3 is your shortcut. The word shortcut could seem lazy, I know, so I hesitate to use it. But we've all taken our fair share of long cuts, haven't we? It was a long cut that brought me to write this chapter. I imagine your own long cuts came with their own boxes and stories that kept you holed up in that box. So let's create a practice that is helpful and efficient as a shortcut for all the days you've spent boxed up on the long road home.

Practice 3: Let There Be Ground, Seed, Grasses, and Trees

This is not the day when God says: let there be a box for humans to hide in. It's the day when what fills the light and watery earth is ground with seed, grasses, and trees. Can you feel the place you've been put? You haven't been boxed in; you've literally been grounded. Notice it. Is gravity in play for you right now? Are you flying off into oblivion, or is it the reality of your physicality that you are grounded? I'm going to make an assumption based on everyone I've ever seen and say that you, like the beautiful trees around you, have your feet on the earth. When you board an airplane, you can do so because of the grounding pull that is exerted in the atmosphere on the plane. Whether gravity is causing your weight to rest in that crowded airplane that you're riding in right now or allowing you to take your shoes off and walk in the grass, you are grounded. Lean in. Feel the weight of your body supported by the earth. You have been rooted like a tree but your roots are not physical; they are electrical. You are a grounded circuit and it's good for you. All around you (I hope) there are trees, plants, seeds in the ground, and grasses, and they are made to sustain life in the most beautiful ways.

This may be the part of the book where you decide that your practice is going to include a drive to the countryside or ten minutes of letting your feet feel the sand underneath them or the grass in the park. It's a big thing on Instagram, the grounding practices, but it's nothing new. This is our design, to be grounded in the earth, and it's for us to thrive with the flow of life in the world. Notice what comes to your mind as you appreciate that there are seeds in the ground about to produce something you cannot yet see. Notice what you appreciate thinking about trees and grasses. Notice what happens when you realize there's a beautiful natural world that you were designed to function with in harmony.

Let's practice.

Say, write, or think as a clear thought: "There is ground, seed, grasses, and trees." Then notice what you notice about what comes to your mind and how you feel.

What do you appreciate about being grounded and taking the time to feel it?

What are you curious about as you feel the weight of your body on the earth?

You are supported. Can you feel it? Your honest answer may be, "Cayce, no, I feel so incredibly unsupported in my life right now! I don't even know where to begin. I'm lost, I'm sad, and I feel all alone." I am not physically with you, but I want to pause and say that it makes sense how you feel. You are not alone in feeling ungrounded, unseen, or isolated. It's a really common feeling. I have felt it so many times.

Take the honesty you are attuned to—good, bad, or ugly and let's take those thoughts and practice again.

Here's where I am and what I feel, honestly (good, bad, ugly—don't judge yourself, show up honest):

Now let's notice the light as you stay in the thoughts above. Just notice them with the addition of light.

Now notice the helpful kind of boundary/separation—God's kind that brings life, clarity, and distinction. Just notice what you notice.

Now notice what you notice as you read this line: "There is ground, seed, and grasses and trees." What do you notice after the "There is" statement? What do you appreciate about what is coming to the screen of your mind?

For years one of the boxes I felt most concretely was a box called "Be a bridge." The main "should" of this box was: I must be the bridge for people. Bridge my friends so everyone gets along. Bridge people to Jesus. Bridge Jesus-people to each other. If I'm walked on repeatedly in the process, it's okay, because connective purposes were at play. It took most of my life to even see how this was a box at all and especially to see how very limiting that box was for me. A lot of great actions came from it, like things I've learned from and would even choose to do again. But the problem with boxes is pretty obvious: to maintain their structural integrity and purpose, you must remain boxed inside.

You and I weren't designed to be a box or live in a box.

You're like a river or a tree, but you are not a cage.

Like a steady stream of cool water that finds its way through an old creek bed. Like the Tigris and Euphrates, said to flank the first garden. Like the Hudson River—at once a source of life to a city and a lifeline runway for a broken plane with a clear-minded pilot. Like the mighty Mississippi forging its way through the middle of a place to craft a nation. Your life is a creative force like a river.

Google tells me that if we stretched out the rivers of blood running through your body at this very moment, your river would flow around the earth twice.

You are not just "like a river" as nice as that simile is. You are a river. While your body does enclose the gory, beautiful, and necessary river that is your insides, it flows. What is deep inside of you produces spiritual, emotional, and physical energy that was always meant to be released freely into the world around you. You need me to flow and I need you to flow. The life inside us was never meant to be dammed up. The life flow is meant to be shared.

Chapter 4—

THE THREAT OF CREATION

Rivers and trees are not easy to box in, control, define, or negate. They can be chopped down and destroyed, but the power of their existence as a species, as part of creation, is not easily dismissed or denied. Their creative energy, power, and potential are a given.

Creativity and I don't just mean artistic creativity, but the act of creating can appear as a threat.

You and I were designed to create; it's innate because we literally *are* creations. We often create things we don't even care about but because our focus and energy is on them, then we find ourselves making choices that revolve around something we don't even care about. But because our thought energy and our time are directed toward them, we will almost always create something involving whatever we are thinking about and showing up for. We create things we didn't even care to create, and that in itself threatens us. We try to blame anything or anyone else. The devil made me do it. My friends were all doing it. Before I knew what was happening, I got caught up in it.

I can create big problems for my family by the way I interact with them, and then I can turn around and create a lie so good I almost believe it myself that goes something like this: they are the problem. For others, the lie shows up like this: I am the problem and if I weren't here things would be better for everyone. It's not art but it requires a modicum of creativity even to engage in lying to ourselves and others and maintaining it. Creative energy in humans abounds; what will we use it for?

We are creative beings for better and worse. Our creativity is made to be filled with light, to bring definition and distinction, and to ground us and bear fruit. It's meant to put beauty on display through our existence, just like the beauty expressed in each day of creation.

Day 4 is no different. Just like the unfathomable beauty of the night sky, the galaxies, and the sunrise, which God said was all quite "good," you and I are beautiful and awe-inspiring by design simply by existing. And we are the ones God called *very* good. They've found that we are made of the same substance as the stars. We are connected in the very fabric of the particles that make us up to the stars hung who knows how long ago in galaxies far, far away.

The beauty and flow of life that you bring wherever you go, is as creative as the night sky. Your flow in collaboration with the flow of those around you is meant to form deep crevices in the earth for even greater and mightier future rivers. You are a river, not a cage. It's time to flow freely and to acknowledge that like it or not, you are creative. Believe it or not, everything about you is creative. See and feel it or not, you are creative. Artsy or not, musical or not, intellectual or not, you are a creative masterpiece like the stars that shine in the universe. It's time to look at how that has subtly threatened you and kept you from embracing the beauty and power of who you are.

When we are threatened by the sheer power of what it is to be created and creative, and to also have the power to create, we will self-limit, self-shame, and create destructive narratives for ourselves. Most often self-destruction is required when we reject our creative powers, which is the opposite of self-expression.

Systems often default to a baseline of self-destruction rather than sitting in the messy middle of what it is to be creative. The choice to view the world through certain lenses is itself an act of creation. If I believe the world to be dangerous, I am looking through a lens that plasters danger onto everything I see, and that in itself will enable a story that is creatively dangerous. I'll feel the feelings of danger as I look at the world, and I'll take action and ingrain habits that solve the problematic lens I have seen so much of my life through called danger. I may not have intentionally chosen this lens. I might have experienced real danger as a kid, and the lens was inadvertently sown into my mental processes. Regardless, it's a creative act. What lenses are actually helpful for us as creative humans who are often threatened by the very reality of our own creativity and the harm it can scare up? For Day 4, the lens we will try on our mind's eye for size is this, "Let there be lights that shine in the sky to serve as signs for the seasons."

Light on Day 1, the sun on Day 4. Heavenly bodies of light, set up to serve at least in part as signs for the seasons? It's an overwhelming thought. It's a unique lens for your life. Let's try it.

Practice 4: Let There Be Lights in the Vault To Serve as Signs for the Seasons

Depending on the translation of the words of Gen. 1, originally written in Hebrew, that you use, you'll find different words for the word "sky." I like the word "vault" because it expresses something of the mystery we all feel about this allegedly ever-expanding universe we exist in. The expanse of the sky is overwhelmingly grand and can just feel plain overwhelming.

Notice where your thoughts are and pick one. You can pick a scenario, a random to-do task from the back corner of your thoughts, a feeling you have, anything. Now notice what you notice about it. Does it come in the form of a picture? Are there feelings attached? Ideas? How does that thought motivate you to action or inaction? Notice it. Now say, write or think about it in the context of the universe—in the setting of all the lights placed in the sky: the sun, the moon, the stars, the galaxies. Notice what you notice in that context. What questions bubble up for you? What do you notice about the season for this thought? What directional thoughts come to mind?

Pick a thought/idea/feeling/scenario and notice what you notice:

Notice this same thought through the lens of the universe—the stars, the moon, the galaxies, the expanse in the sky...

What are you curious about? Ask it, remember to practice dialogue-style thinking rather than monologue:

What do you notice about the season for this thought? What do you sense about direction?

Ask: How has being creative appeared as a threat to me?

> Ask: What is real about my creative power?

How has being creative threatened you? If you think you are not creative, it's a good sign that who you are designed to be not only threatens you but you have in some way shut it down. Remember, that doesn't mean you have actually been successful at shutting it down. The reality is that you are constantly moving in a form of creative energy, and you just might not define it as "creative." People caught in cycles of addiction must remain endlessly creative to sustain the momentum of their life. People who are violent and abusive must employ many creative faculties to maintain not only their sanity but their story so that they avoid the devastating consequences of their actions. Try as we may to shut down our creative way of being, what we actually shut down is the enjoyment of our creativity and its directive function. You and I create. Until we own this and dismantle the threat, we will default into a form of dismissive, wandering creativity that does not direct our lives in the ways it was intended to. We miss out on the enjoyment that we were designed to experience by exercising our own powerful creative flow. To live a life with unembraced creativity is a deep self-rejection and it robs those around us of potential beauty, wisdom, and inspiration.

There is a certain type of Christian theology that insists all agree that we are sinful and fallen as humans. It insists on a narrative called original sin insinuating that after Eve and Adam ate the fruit from the forbidden tree, all of creation has been completely defiled. If the words "absolute depravity of man" don't ring a bell for you, you can thank your lucky stars (wink, wink, it's Day 4!). For some of us, we were taught that all humans are wholly depraved due to original sin and what happens in the chapters that follow creation, Genesis 2-4. I don't bring this up to argue against it, though I could. I bring it up as an example of the creative power of humans who did not die off post-Genesis 1. The narrative that we are nothing but wrong and depraved creates something. As a kid and teen, I watched this narrative create a whole generation of shut-down human children of God who deeply questioned their validity and worthiness. Create self-ownership and expression? Not even on the table because of the power created by the story of what I call "capital S" sin. Do you see where there's room for "acceptable" creativity? Yes, in fighting against a sin nature. In arguing about who's right or wrong, in or out based on theological correctness. In making sure that others don't think too much of themselves or "steal God's glory" as if that was even possible.

I grew up with this propaganda. You can imagine my surprise when I started listening in on hundreds of people's conversations with God (note: these are actual sessions of people listening to God's voice, having two-way conversations with Jesus, and processing that in a healthy way, not sessions of people talking about what they *think* about God). I expected God's voice to remind people of what I had learned and believed my whole life about how sinful and untrustworthy we humans were. It has never happened. Not once have I heard God affirm this theology. Quite the opposite. When someone comes in and has a thought somewhere in the vein of, "I'm nothing, not worth anything but God loves me." They hear a reply more in this territory, "You're not nothing because I made you and in me is everything good, especially you. You come from me and I am love, so you're full of love. I do love you and I'll help you learn to love yourself, we have some work to do there." That last phrase is about as pointed as I hear God get. God's voice is surprisingly good, better than everyone expects. No matter where people come into two-way prayer theologically—it matters none as they actually have a real conversation with God. God knows how to speak kindly to the hardest hearts. Where have I seen the hardest hearts you ask? Not in the "lost" or "pagan" world as I was taught as a kid. It's always the most religious and theologically concerned that have the hardest time actually hearing and receiving the loving voice of God. What happens when I get to sit in on a prayer session with someone who doesn't even know what they think about God but is open? It's spiritual alchemy—holy ground. Those are the times that feel so real, honest, and holy that my natural inclination is to want to take my shoes off, to say very little, and I can do nothing else but stand amazed at the beauty of how God connects with every single one of us.

Beware the power of your creativity. It can create for you the illusion of a world that is far harsher and limiting than the one that was actually created for you to live in. How do you begin to dismantle the threat? Just a glance at the night sky will do it. What do you appreciate most when you see the stars and the faint outline of the Milky Way galaxy? And to think, you're made of that same stardust. You may not be exactly the same as what you see up there, but you are as creative, as magnificent, and as glorious. You will not escape your creativity, so look at what you are creating. What is being magnified through you? Beauty? Brokenness? Pain? Pleasure? Power? Control? Humility? Honor? Art? Connection? Hiddenness? Judgment? Boxes? Lines? Right/wrong? Justice? Jealousy? Authenticity? Joy? Belonging? Rejection? Shame? Compassion? Empathy? Wisdom? Freedom? Play? Vision?

It's an easy switch to flip and the road to freedom is marked with honesty, noticing what you notice, and staying curious in dialogue. Try it out on yourself, try it out on God, and/or try it out on a trusted friend. Notice what that kind of alchemy feels like to your mind, to your heart, and to your body.

Chapter 5—

THE THREAT OF REPRODUCTION

I've always heard that copying is the highest form of flattery but I never bought it. I was way too insecure to admit that. I have always loved design, color, and the interplay between the two. So if someone picks a design I love whether for their home, their wardrobe, or their family, internally, I check it off the list as no longer an option. Why? Because I have a weird fear about reproducing instead of producing. I was terrified as a ten year old writing my first papers in school that I would somehow inadvertently plagiarize—that, in my mind, would make me the "defrauding poster child." Even for this book, I pretty much stopped reading other books and listening to most podcasts because of this internal drive to not be a copy, to be an original. I also want to be relevant—in the best sense, to create in ways that actually mean something to people and practically impart something good to them. In a lesser sense, I want everyone to like me. I've been a people pleaser to the max.

How does the threat of reproduction show up? Comparison, people pleasing, an obsession with being original, fear of being wrong or saying/doing something wrong that someone else might copy. There are others, that's just the most familiar territory for me. Here's the thing: like creativity, reproduction is just built into the scenario of what it is to be a human. Just like you learned in health class as a kid, you have a reproductive system and that's just the start. Every part of you is being recreated currently to replace the old cell that is getting tired even as we speak. You are a living, breathing replication waiting to happen. You will reproduce. You do reproduce even if you never have human offspring.

If we can make peace with this threat, embracing the replicative, multiplicable nature of our humanity—dismantling all that it triggers in us to think about what that might mean (does it really have to mean anything? Notice the story in your head there.). Then we can embrace what is. Embrace it and you will naturally replicate it.

What you care about will spread like wildfire, somewhere. Your children will become who you are. Your workplace will quietly espouse both your strengths and your weaknesses. You will create followers, whether you are aware of it or not. There is a common foe to enjoying the built-in superpower of replication: the voice of lack.

Lack tells us that something is missing or broken with something or some person. For most of us, at the core, lack tells the same story that I mentioned in the last chapter. I latched on for dear life to this story of lack at a certain point in my development. It was taught to me by my people (yes, highly religious neo-Calvinist friends are my people). It's the story that humans are sorely lacking. In some circles, the words coined are "absolute depravity"—*strong* language.

I believed it hook, line, and sinker. The narrative is that there is absolutely something horribly wrong with all humans - full depravity. There's a little something true in there, right? In our immaturity, hurt, and disillusionment, we all can make huge messes causing harm to ourselves and each other. But there's also something highly incomplete about the idea. It doesn't jive with the overarching story from the beginning to today about God's work in the world.

God didn't create trash. This is just one example of how the narrative of lack takes hold. It's a very obvious example even an easy target. But before you take aim at the evangelical Christians (man they/we are really lacking! ;), this is *what we all do* in one way or another. It's not always so overt, but to be a human is to experience a lacking narrative about something! Ourselves, God and/or the world around us—just as Eve did in her "perfect state." The very human tendency to default into thinking something is majorly wrong and lacking, with you, me, us, the world, or "them," whoever they are is the human condition.

Calvinists would have a point here to argue that it's "original sin"—the state may be accurate if we can drop the interpretation that follows. We get lost in this interpretation. We then decided that something's wrong and we have to do something about it to fix what was lacking in the first place. But the lie is in the label "lack." Eve and Adam experienced a very real curiosity or questioning or doubt before they ate the fruit—what does that tell us? What if it's okay?. What if it's helpful to understand that this too may be a very important part of the design? Maybe it's an important part of development that will actually get us into the really important narrative of our life—discovery, development, embodiment, creativity, reproduction/replication, communion, and rest. These are beautiful things we get to learn in life. No human was ever born entered the world perfectly complete and mature, not even the garden couple themselves. The actual story of our lives that involves *growing love and appreciation for life* is the one that will always overshadow and overwhelm the underwhelming story of lack, fear, and shame.

Lack, fear and shame are not our identity. We were not born into them. We do experience them and that's part of life. Of life for you, to grow you, to move you out of harm's way, to indicate that there's pain or trauma that needs healing. Shame, fear, and lack are nothing to hide from. They are so useful if you will let them draw you into the greater narrative of connection. You can talk about these things with trusted people and find freedom. You can take your mental dialogue with shame or fear and start talking to God about it and as you embody a broader narrative—the false threat of these feelings will give way to the experience of gratitude for your amazing ability to process them and replicate those new thoughts in such a way that you are building new brain ruts and new options for yourself!

The narrative of Day 5 of creation tells the story of diversity and abundance—*it is what is*. Diversity and abundance exist throughout creation, and if we can honor it in the created world around us, we will know it and experience it in ways that will forever outpace our ability to argue the merits of it. Explaining why something is beautiful and good is much easier after it's been experienced as beautiful and good. Then the language has a place to land. This is how we grow best: experience it before creating a label. Labels are powerful when experiential knowledge is there. Without experience first, labels mostly create structures that rise and fall by consensus on who is most right.

Can you imagine what it's like to catalog all the fish in the sea? The birds, all of them, in the air? Even in this day of Google searches and chatGPT (is it still a thing now?). The data on sea creatures and our winged birds of a feather who flock together is bountiful. It's abundant. Not lacking.

Practice 5: There Is Abundance

Take any thought or scenario, especially one that feels limiting. Where are you struggling to find solutions or freedom or a way forward?

First, you'll write out the story that scenario is telling you and all the problems that come attached to it.

Second, you'll hold it with an open hand—that open hand up signifies for you now that you are willing to receive abundance in all the areas that felt limiting and perplexing.

Third, you'll ask this question: What if I wasn't lacking anything and had everything I needed right now?

Fourth, ask abundance what the true story is. You can even say, "Lack said this: (write it out)." Then add, "But abundance says this: write it out)."

*If you feel stuck in the voice and narrative of lack and it's hard for you to feel or hear anything but that, you may want to jump to the Out of the Box practice and the Hearing God practice. Sometimes it really helps to ask questions directly to God and notice what comes to mind immediately afterward. It will get you unstuck.

Write out the story of your thought/scenario that's lacking:

Picture holding it with an open hand and placing it into abundance. Then notice what you notice:

Ask this question: What if I wasn't lacking anything and had everything I needed right now?

"Lack said this: (read the top box). But abundance says this: (write it out)."

When we're reproducing anything important to us, whether that's human offspring, a business model, an event, our values, or our legacy, the opportunity can become threatening and overwhelming in a surprisingly short period of time because we care.

In 2008 or 2009 I was working on a few of these care-driven endeavors. I had two babies under age three and one on the way. I was thinking about starting a bridesmaid dress business with my best friend Kim. I was deeply invested in a few other places in our community and I was worried. I was worried that by continuing to work and adding more to my plate I'd be a bad mom. I was concerned that I was shirking responsibility on both ends trying to run a new business and having a newborn. Someone close to me had made a comment about whether or not I really had time for work at this juncture in my life.

All these thoughts were swirling when in the middle of the night, our second son, Hudson, who was still in a crib at the time, woke up crying. With young kids I wasn't one to rush in and stay in forever. My goal was usually to comfort and then leave them to fall back asleep on their own. But this night was a little bit different. I was feeling sentimental about the fact that he wouldn't be that small or rockable forever. Instead of rocking him for a minute or two and laying him back down, I just held on and rocked and sang. I lost track of time, but somewhere in there, my thought pattern went along these lines, wavering between a train of thought and prayer: "I love these kids so much. What I really want for Hudson as he grows up is for him to become exactly who *he* is. I don't want him to become who I want him to be or who his grandparents think he should be or who anyone says he should be. I just want him to be who he is, and who God made him to be. I don't want him to ever apologize for that (In the midst of my wish/prayer mental monologue, a thought jumped in making it a dialogue). "That's exactly the same way I feel about you, Cayce." I sensed the Spirit of God say to me, "Your kids won't be great because you spent every single minute with them. They aren't great because you are constantly there (you'll always be there plenty). They become who you are."

I knew with that short phrase *they become who you are*, that my best parenting would not come from my micromanaging presence but from me becoming the fullest version of myself I could become. I so desperately wanted Hudson to become Hudson, intuiting for him that *that* was best for him. So the best I could do was model it. For me, the decision to work and open that business and others were not as much about time management or income, as it was about being who I am and pursuing things that bring me life. Giving myself permission to become me without apology even if it was very different from the way my mom and her mom had done it was an important breakthrough for me in this area of reproduction. I could spend every waking moment with my kids and feel better about myself, but it guaranteed nothing about how they would turn out. There was something more important. We will reproduce who we are, not what we hope for, dictate, or control. This is the heart of mentorship, and in the Christian world, the heart of the word people use for spiritual fathering/mothering/mentorship is discipleship.

The whisper of God that day to me shifted something internally around my own personal integrity. It was a nudge in the direction of self-awareness and the value of my personal self-expression that I desperately needed. The message was also this: Cayce, try to control less what you can't (who Hudson becomes) and more of what you can: who you are. Freedom rushed in. Relief replaced anxiety. It wasn't because I felt I had permission to ditch my kids (parents might joke here, but that's never what we would actually ever want). In the permission to still "be me" and pursue the things I love outside of being a mom, I felt permission to relate to my kids for the rest of their lives from a different paradigm that had far more to do with living fully and valuing our shared humanity than it did with getting something just right or looking right.

Later I would learn an official term for that egoic pursuit to have to get it right and look like we have gotten it right and have it all together even though internally we might be abandoning ourselves: narcissism.

I know that the threat is real when we care because we want the best. But in our pursuit of the best, if we abandon integrity we will find everything lacking: ourselves, others, time, God, and our life circumstances. But when we can see that what is real is not what's lacking or the story of lack, but that there's abundance all around us, the threat is dismantled.

As I enjoyed rocking Hudson that night, I felt the abundance that arises from the freedom of choice. This freedom is always there and when we can lean in, life will reproduce both freedom and abundance in spades like the great multipliers that they are. Control is an illusion that's just about addition. Lack is about subtraction. *Abundance is multiplicable.* There was enough time to rock Hudson for as long as I wanted that night and there was enough time for me to be myself in life and be a great mom too. No, there wasn't enough time for me to try to be everything to everyone (a lesson I would learn the hard way later), but there was abundantly more than enough time and space in life for those two things.

Chapter 6—

THE THREAT OF COMMUNION

The Story of Little Bulldog Bird: Out of the bird's nest, into the chicken coop.

There once was a bird, we'll call him "Little Bird" who thought he was a bulldog.

The bird "growled" at strangers, mainly the local chickens. The ants passing by found this to be quite odd and ineffective.

Little Bird took it upon himself to keep the chickens in the coop. "I must!" He thought to himself often. See, that's what his neighbor, the bulldog, did every day.

Little Bird bravely mustered all he could muster to stand guard and stop the chickens from going out to pasture. Let me pause here and warn you that this story does not end well for our bird. The whole story is rife with tragedy.

After many attempts to keep the chickens in, the chickens and Little Bird learned that the fastest way for the chickens to get to the pasture was simply by trampling Little Bird.

He experienced little to no success keeping the chickens in the coop although he was, in fact, doing all the same things that he saw Bulldog do.

The thing that most birds do was the thing that our Little Bird simply did not know how to do: fly away freely.

To understand the actions of Baby Bird, we must understand his mindset. His mindset functioned like a lockbox constructed long, long ago.

Little Bird was hatched in a tree placed strategically above Bulldog's pen. Wise Mama Bird observed that none in the animal kingdom dared to ruffle Bulldog's feathers. "What an ideal place for a feathered home!" she thought, where no intruder dared to engage.

Strategically birthed above Bulldog, safety ensured, Baby Bird entered happily into a world of nested feathers. Mama Bird took great comfort in knowing that her babies would live and not die thanks to Bulldog below. Mama Bird did not anticipate the impending tragic accident that would change everything.

Headed out to search for dinner, Mama Bird flew directly into a neighboring tree limb. She plunged headlong to her eternal rest beneath the tree beside Bulldog's favorite spot to nap. Baby Bird did not remember seeing his mama fly, but there was no forgetting the fall.

Thankfully, this particular Bulldog had a healthy respect for life and death. Baby Bird peered out of the nest in time to see Bulldog nudge his mother to the nearby bushes. Then he watched as Bulldog scared off the animals who came to sniff out her carcass. Baby Bird, so new to the world, determined this one thing and one thing only: "I must get to the ground to live among the bushes."

All that Baby Bird wanted, naturally, was to be near his mama where he belonged.

What Baby Bird set his mind to was as good as done. After a big tumble to the ground, Baby Bird made a home in the shade of the bushes, coming out only to peck at a roly-poly or snatch the head of an earthworm. This worked fine for a while for Baby Bird but it did not work in this specific way: Baby Bird did not know and could not see that as a bird, he was not made for the bushes.

Baby Bird soon discovered he was alone in the world and was quick in his grieving to appreciate the ways of the Bulldog. As Baby Bird grew into Little Bird, his admiration for Bulldog turned into emulation. Though the ways of a Bulldog would normally seem very curious for a bird, to Little Bird, they were normal.

In reality, Bulldog was much *bigger* than Little Bird, but the bird didn't notice. Bulldog was much *louder* than the bird, so our bird did his best to sing in a lower octave.

Bulldog influenced the other animals, even giving them directions.

"Grrr, grr, grr, ruff ruff, growl," he murmured in a low tone. At his growl, the chickens scrambled to their hen house.

"Grrrrrrrrr, rrr, rrrrurrrurrrurr, grrrrrrururr," and the possum would cower by the fence.

"Grrrrrrr. Rwaaaaarrrrr, rrrrr, rufff," and all the neighboring cows would take notice of Bulldog's intentions.

You know this story. You know what happens to a little bird who tries to use the tactics of a bulldog to survive and thrive in life. It just doesn't work.

Little Bird huffed and puffed but no walls were ever blown down.

On a good day, Little Bird was ignored. On a bad day, he was maimed.

Yet on no day did our "bulldog" of a bird actually become a bulldog.

And more tragic still, on no day did Little Bird discover he had his very own set of wings.

The pain of being trampled was almost too much to bear until it simply was too much to bear.

If only Little Bird knew he was made to fly. Little Bird had a traumatic start: identity issues, a mindset issue, and multiple gaps in his training. Though most of these complications were indeed predicated on early tragedy and loss, the facts remain: a bird is made to fly—meant for the wide open skies.

There's a part of Little Bird in all of us.

Some of us have been working really hard to prove that we are something or someone other than ourselves. It's not that we're afraid of ourselves, but early on we became weary of our own design and we stopped trusting the wings we were given. Perhaps we are completely unaware of certain God-given elements of our design.

Some of us have been terrified that our desire to soar was wrong and reserved only for the special, beautiful, strong birds—the ones with a family or at least flight coaches to point the way.

Some of us have been soaring for years but have lost appreciation for wings that work and just how far they can take us.

Every human has a version of Little Bird's story to tell. When we forget who we are, likely for good reason, we then find ourselves grounded, stuck, or worse yet, trampled by what seems like inevitable circumstances.

How we have interpreted the past, the stories we tell ourselves about our lives now, and the stories we believe about the lives of those around us create invisible boxes making flight a forgotten destiny.

You're a river, not a cage.

You're made to be a human, not God.

You're designed to be who you are but when that image is repressed or not reflected back to you well, you will naturally experience identity amnesia and all the frustration that comes with it.

While only you can live your life and express your own core identity in the world, you and I are uniquely dependent upon each other to see ourselves—to reflect back to us who we are. Did you know that your eyes have these things called mirror neurons in them where you are reflected back to yourself when you look into other people's eyes? It's an essential part of our growth to have eye-to-eye contact as a baby and eye-to-eye connection as we continue to grow. We need one another and will forever be interdependent. Compassion connects us and keeps us aware of our forever connection as members of the family we call humanity. Codependence comes from a lack of authentic affection and loving attention. Codependency comes from the control and fear of abandonment that arises when we fall from the nest and think we are all alone in a bulldog world.

What does this have to do with communion? Let's take the word as it is. Com—with. Union—connection, togetherness, belonging, integration, oneness.

There are three broad relational facets to communion and they can all show up as a threat. We say that we want a connection with people, and deep down I know we all really do. But as life happens and things hurt, we can easily hide behind the fear of getting hurt or the lack of trust we have experienced when it comes to these three all-important relationships.

1. Comm-union with self.

2. Comm-union with Source (God, Creator, Spirit—I don't use "universe" because I'm talking about the entity beyond the creation, behind it, sourcing it).

3. Comm-union with creation (each other, other people groups, other cultures, those who've come before us and those we leave behind, nature, the world, the universe).

Integrity is far more than being a person of your word. To be integral connotes an inner integration inside of oneself. That inner integration, because we are spiritual beings, will inevitably lead to the exploration of an inner spiritual connection or integration with Spirit. I do not mean this in the way that I've heard many religious leaders speak of it: something to do—"get connected to God." What I'm talking about is in the realm of discovering what is actually real: you are connected to your Source. Whether or not you speak to your biological mother and father or not, you remain connected in a deeply spiritual way.

Whatever you choose to believe about this doesn't change the fact that you were birthed into a specific family. You may also have relationally connected with others in the human family and you may experience your connection to them in a stronger way than even your own birth parents. Regardless, your source connection is inextricably linked to who you are as a human. As it is in the physical, far more so spiritually. You are connected to your Creator, even if you don't feel it or know it as a reality yet. All of spirituality and even all of your material physical experiences (yes, everything is spiritual) will ultimately affirm what is.

Truth is truth regardless of what we think of it. Part of that truth is that you are powerfully connected to life through the power of your communication central, your mind. When your powerful mind believes you are disconnected from God and others, the sheer powerful nature of you makes the thought have weight in the world, at least temporarily. You can live into a false narrative about your life (i.e., I'm separate from God. I'm disconnected from others. I live in a vacuum unaffected by others and not affecting others) and that false narrative will seem true to a certain extent because of the creative power of your thoughts.

When the basic and ungrounded feeling of isolation creeps in, it's like the basic metal of your life. When isolation gets isolated in your mind, it becomes a reality for you. It's a powerful reality that you can experience even when surrounded by many people. *Here's where we need to flip the switch*. Ask yourself, am I really alone? See what answers pop up immediately for you. Some may challenge the thought that you are alone. Others will affirm it. You may have spent so much time feeling alone (like Little Bird) that the thought of flying with a flock of birds sounds completely unattainable, as unrealistic as a fairy tale.

False narratives hold up because of the power of your mind. What do we do when we don't have or experience comm-union within? What do I mean? I'm talking about what happens when we self-reject because we think part of us is bad or because someone in authority told us we were born in sin (true, there are all kinds of brokenness you can experience in life) and are totally depraved (wait for a second, is that what it says in Genesis 1–3, totally? Depraved? Hmm, what happened to good, very good, and made in the image of God?). Maybe it wasn't theological but was still very experiential. Maybe we self-rejected when we thought all the kids in the class were laughing at us, or when your mom said you were on her last nerve.

Regardless of how it happened, it's a common reality of being a human that, at least in part, we judge ourselves as wrong and then we get busy trying to prove that we can be right (ego development 101). This is essential and not "bad;" it just is. We become afraid and ashamed and then we think we are afraid and we are shameful. And this un-reality sure functions like reality and before we know it, we have divorced ourselves from parts of ourselves that are essential and undivorceable. So it doesn't work, it just feels like we are a big splinter. The truth is, we are one—every interior part of us is deeply integrated and connected. As integrated as we are internally as a human being, we are as deeply connected to those we came from: both Creator and mother/father/family. We are not and never have been alone or disconnected, not really. Do you see how the threat here is not actually separation or disintegration? We're used to thinking like that. We hide in it. What really threatens us is what could be real about us: we are communion. We are one. You are within those parts you want to hide and shame; they are you. We are, you and I, as different as we may act and believe ourselves to be. We are inextricably connected as part and parcel of one another, humankind. As much as I may want to believe in God, do believe in God, don't, or am mad at God, it changes nothing about what is real. What is, is.

You are not shame, shame is shame. You are you and if part of you feels shame, you cannot shame it away. What is, is. The shame thought can be turned on its head and dismissed. The part of you that feels shame cannot. Learning to tell the difference between yourself and shame, between others and shame, and between God and shame is the name of the game when it comes to using your mind to bring about the gold of your life.

Practicing mind alchemy is about using the inquisitive, conversational nature of our thought life to discover what is real about all of life: communion.

Until this point, we have practiced flipping the mental switch on any thought by using our innate (whether you knew it or not) communion with creation to think differently. Light. God's kind of separation. Grounding. The Cosmos. Abundance.

For dismantling the threat of communion, the actual practice of communion we already have access to is essential. This can happen simply by asking yourself relational dialoguing questions and listening to your own answers because God made you with a wise and brilliant mind, heart, and body. Listening to them flips a switch internally. How do we practice having a conversation with God? A form of communion, arguably an incredibly powerful form.

It's as easy as thinking. Prayer for most is one direction, shooting questions and concerns or gratitude into the proverbial heavens. Hoping, and truly believing often, that it will land somewhere that matters "in the big guy's lap."

It's nice but problematic in so many ways.

1. God's not a big guy. (Male and female they created us, in their image. It's both/and).

2. God's not way up there. Immanuel means with us. The overarching story of God throughout human history has been of a God that communes with us, near, at hand, spirit, breath, as close as that very breath you are taking.

3. Prayer is not wishful thinking requiring blind faith in the invisible.

So before we talk about "Hearing God" or prayer, please take note of these caveats:

1. Anyone can hear God anytime because of your humanity. You don't need to figure out everything right about God and pass a test.

2. I don't mean the crazy version of hearing God that's filled with awkward judgment and holier-than-thou, future-predicting hoopla.

3. I'll show you how. Just try it before you dismiss it.

4. Be honest. If you try this, you need to be honest with yourself and note what comes to mind even if you think it's not "God." You can sort that out later.

5. Understand that this practice will change your life gently and kindly. It's for everyone, it's easy, and I'm happy to teach you, but don't think you'll ever be the same after a little practice. You will find out that connection and union—communion is real, built in, and it will melt everything down into a river of life- giving energy that is hard to turn back from. Just a warning.

6. Don't walk around saying stupid things like, "God told me (fill in the blank), it means (fill in the blank), and therefore you should (fill in the blank)." This is a violation on so many levels. If you want to practice finding the place where every human can have conversations with God personally, great—but be humble about the practice. Say things like, "Here's what I got when I asked this question…Here's what it could mean. Here's what I'm gonna do or not do." Don't shirk your bad or good choices onto God by saying He told you to…how about owning your own decisions? Don't be dogmatic and act like you have to be right…when you practice two-way prayer or hearing God's voice, you might get it wrong and

that's okay. If you're willing to be wrong and open to input, you won't do dumb stuff that is the opposite of God's love and life force in the world. You will not be that person who says God told you to bomb an abortion clinic or something crazy. You'll recognize that for what it is: harmful.

So here are the basics on how to get started in a non-scary way:

Practice the communion you have with God. Start by recognizing that your breath, keeping you alive now, came from a place. Maybe that's enough for today. Listen to the breath that's coming into your lungs and going out. Listen for the sound of your heartbeat. This life is coming from somewhere. It's been given to you. Can you feel that God is as close as your breath physically? Can you let that nearness comfort you?

Ready to try more? Think about your thoughts. They all end up in the territory of story and conversation. Interpreting our experiences and conversing—*dialoguing*—about them. You are always in a dialogue if you slow down your thoughts and look at them, with *something* or *someone*.

1. Yourself

2. The past

3. The future

4. A feeling: shame, fear, insecurity, joy, hope, aspirations

5. Ideas, passions, visions, dreams

6. People (could be rehashing the conversation you had three weeks ago that went wonky and triggered you or it could just be the voice of a good friend replaying in your mind).

7. God

I put number one, you, and number seven, God as bookends because there are two entities that will remain with you in your mind always whether you acknowledge them or not. You and God. The others come and go. The others are not "who" you are but they are connected to you and that's why you dialogue with them. Some are for your benefit, others less so; they're just seemingly stuck there.

The space you get to tend is the you/God space. It's a really creative space and it's the space of Practice 6. It's like a beautiful garden. It's a fertile place for all kinds of creation to seed and sprout.

People often worry when they start practicing hearing God, "What if it's just me?" I'm not worried at all about that because if it's really the real you talking, you're a chip off the old block and it will be in harmony with what God would say. The question to ask is, "What's not me and what's not God?" That's more important for tilling the soil of your mind. If, when thinking about your thoughts, you notice lots of shame thoughts sprouting up, you can pull them into a conversation with God. If you notice lots of fear thoughts or just plain old mindset thoughts springing up, you can take a look at that with God in the space of co-creation or conversation: turning something over together with another.

The space where you can always find God's voice and your authentic voice is in the way you already think. Think about the way your thoughts already sound. You have been taking the time to notice them throughout this whole book. How do they come to you? Some come in the form of feelings first, then words, and even little movie memories in the mind. Other times, the picture pops to mind first, then a little movie or "vision" plays on the screen of your mind chock full of imagery and ideas, and then words and feelings. Intuition is a form of feeling and idea combined. The same way you *already* think is the same way you'll "hear" God or better said, receive communication from God. Paying attention to what comes on the screen of your mind is the key.

God's voice will *not* sound like a man's booming voice from the movies. God's voice will not sound "'other" to you, because it's actually quite familiar. I promise you've already heard God's voice in your life but you likely took credit for it as your own, which is just fine.

Okay, let's practice. Remember, note what comes to your mind and be honest. Act like you are dictating the "ticker tape" of your own mind and don't dismiss anything initially.

You talk to God just like you would talk to any other person/entity: directly. Just in this case, you can do it in your head if you want to. If it helps you to write it out or say it out loud that's fine too. Questions work best and how do you ask a normal person a question? You direct it their way, "Hey Joe, are you here?" And if they are there, you'll get a response pretty quickly. Well God is near so that's an easy one to ask. Just practice noticing the response that comes to mind, and don't dismiss it as, "Oh, I just made that up." Try it out. (One more thing, I ask Jesus a lot of questions because that is truly honest for me. I know Jesus and God and Spirit to be one and the same with different expressions. But even in Jesus' day, no one called him that because they didn't speak English and that name didn't exist (they called him the Hebrew name "Yeshua"), so let's not get hung up on names. You may not know what you think about Jesus so it would feel false to address Jesus, so use the word that honors what is real for you and comfortable for you around God. What matters is not the name but the intention to dialogue and discover what is real.)

Ask in your thoughts or out loud, *God, are you with me?* Now notice and record the very first thing that pops into your mind (remember you're practicing dialogue not monologue so capture the "answer" that sounds like you but hold space for it to actually be God's still small voice there in your mind). Put down the first thing that comes and then ask the next logical question that you have. Then record, again, the very first thing that comes to mind after you ask the direct next question of God. What do you notice as you practice this? What happened? This is what I love to coach people in because I've never met anyone that I can't help find the voice of God if they really want to find it. It's there already, which makes it easy. I just help people recognize where to find it and access it.

Let's do another practice.

Practice 6: Co-creating with God/Moving with God

In this case, the moving and co-creating we'll do is in the form of a narrative story of a mental journey. You'll see what I mean after we practice it.

I'll ask the questions of God for you so you can just read them, and then notice what comes to your mind next and record it. Once you do that, then go back and check to see if it sounds like God. Here's how God sounds: loving, kind, life-giving, encouraging, freedom-bringing, healing, restoring, redeeming, convicting (meaning kindness that changes the way we think and act for good). Here's what's *not* God: shaming, condemning, accusing, things that sound like kill/steal/destroy, shoulds/oughts, or "religious" answers that imply separation, depressing, lacking, frustrating. After you do your conversation and record your listening for God, then you can go back and check it out. If it doesn't come from love and produce love in you when you hear it, either chunk it and don't call it "God's voice" or ask God about it and why it came up. Let it go if it's anything that sounds like accusation, shame, or lack. If God's answers stir up a question for you like, "What the heck does that mean?" or "What does that represent?" great, ask it!

God, remind me of a time when I felt peace: (Describe what jumps into your mind however significant or insignificant it seems.)

Note the time of day, season, location, colors, feelings, all the things you can sense with your senses, and your impression of what's coming to mind:

Note what you appreciate about the memory:

God, where are you in this memory? (Note where you sense God's presence/what's highlighted to you as you read the question):

God, why did you bring this memory to mind?

God, what do you want me to know from your heart to mine right now?

Now look back at what you got as you described what came to mind imme-diately after asking God the questions. Check it. Does it sound like the "what God sounds like" side of things? If not, maybe you chunk it and chalk it up to what you had for lunch coming out. Or maybe it actually does sound loving and encouraging in a way you don't normally talk to yourself. Hold onto that. Maybe you just have questions. Take note of them. Maybe something came up that sounded more like an old religious accusation or "rule." That's interesting, what honest question does that bring to mind for you? Ask that directly to God and note what comes to mind next. Check that answer, How does it feel to you? Does it resonate with you?

Chapter 7–

THE THREAT OF REST

In my forties, five kids in, and many jobs later, it's easy to laugh a little at this one. Are you threatened by rest? It's what I've wanted my whole life. True.

Also, not true, not fully.

Deep down, in the realm of what we really really want, when we are honest with ourselves, we all want rest. We all want to be able to be cared for, to let our guard down, to surrender, knowing we are cared for and loved. Enough of *that* kind of rest for our souls sparks energy within that can actually cause us to soar. A genuine form of energy that has ease, grace, and joy attached to it. Then why does it show up as a threat?

It obviously threatens our ego, the part of us that must appear to know it all, to do it all "right" and to be an integral part of solutions for good (whatever we think that looks like). Our ego does not like the idea of real rest because rest dismantles the ego. I don't know who first said E.G.O stands for edging God out, and I think that's a helpful way to think of it, but I'd add to that: ego is our greatest attempt to be like God without the healthy understanding we already are. Ego says you must get it right (be God), be perfect, be on the right side, do right, look right, be smart, not be deceived, and not mess it up.

The ego always comes from our very human, normal concern that we are lacking or missing something and we need to make up for that. What happens when we edge God out of the equation of our minds? We think we are lacking and need to make up for it. Subconsciously we think we must be God. We must be the one to keep all the plates spinning, to fix the world, to heal, to perfect, to perform, to please, we must at all costs play God. But it doesn't work. The amount of control we need to exert betrays our own heart's desire to connect and love. The pressure we put on ourselves and others to get our acts together ends up driving deep wedges into the natural connections we share as humans. It's inescapable. That's the story of Eve in the garden, to think that we are missing something, that we are lacking, even when we have been given everything. Eve had it all. Adam, the garden, all of it, and most impressively, Eve had a free-flowing interaction with God as desired. Relational union and empowered identity: humans.

Join Me in this garden to bless, multiply, and fill the earth with Me, God says to His/Her children. And even then, they thought they were missing something and needed to get what they already had the whole time. "Be like God? I need that!" But they already were!

The story is mine and yours and it's a perfect picture of what happens to every human on their journey. We try to attain something significant to prove that we are as valuable as we always were but didn't know. We think we are lacking. We search for the missing pieces. Our ego constructs a big plan about how best to do this and which pitfalls to avoid all the while trying to be like God or even our own little god, to find out we were born into it all along.

Can we rest from trying so hard to get what we already have? Enoughness.

Can we feel that the way we were made and who we are is what we are actually seeking? Can we accept that rest is built in for us (sleep for starters)? Communion is our very real energetic state. Reproduction happens.

Creativity and making creations happen by design or default for us as humans. We were born to discover and that's how we grow; all the questions are good questions. Development can't be stopped. That seed sprouting right up through the concrete thing is real! We have been embodied—the more-than-enough spirit of who you are actually gets to be in a body of amazing flesh and bones, and you get to have physical experiences. It's the chance of a lifetime, and yes, it comes with pain and pleasure—the best of teachers.

Can we rest from worrying so much about mitigating these things and just receive the gift that it is to be a human being made in God's image rather than constantly trying to be God, who we're not?

There are two trees highlighted in the garden of Genesis among many others. One is life and it's for the humans to eat from. The other is judgment and it's really overwhelming for the humans. This is God's tree. The fruit is not what we want to bear but the story tells us something so important about the human journey. We all try the fruit out; it's what it is to be human: to try living as judge and jury first and foremost of ourselves. We judge ourselves to be lacking and then we take the weight of the world on to become enough but it never is quite enough, is it?

Rest will save our lives. The whole creation story will. If we can let our minds bask in the light, and experience the kind of division and boundaries that bring beauty and distinction and connection. If we can feel the ground under our feet and reset our whole nervous system on occasion. If we can look up and get lost in the stars and follow their lead. If we can see, feel, and appreciate the immense built-in abundance that surrounds us. If we can move with God because God's never been far from any single one of us. If we can let it go and rest, cease our striving, we will become real boys and real girls—humans created to share a space that's vibrant and thriving, teeming with life.

Let's practice!

Practice 7: Be the Seed

A wise friend and teacher once said, "Unless a grain of wheat falls into the earth and dies, it remains alone; but if it dies, it bears much fruit."[4] My friend and coworker Rosalind, who leads One Journey Retreats with me, leads a section called the seed and the husk. She reads the quote above and then reminds us that the seed doesn't actually die when it hits the ground, the husk does. There's a husk around the seed that comes off and eventually melds into the dirt. The seed gets exposed and buried in the cool womb of fertile soil. What happens next is an incredible picture of self-expression, creativity, replication. and abundance: fruitfulness.

Let's listen to God about this. Notice what you notice:

> God, bring to mind an area of my life that could use some rest.

---

4.   John 12:24 (ESV).

God, what does it look like to let go and release?

God, what's the husk?

God, what's the seed?

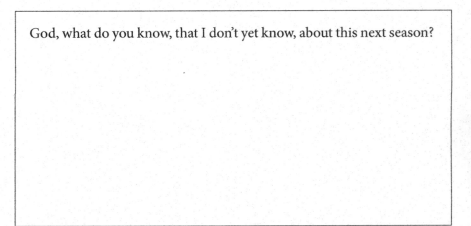

God, what's happening in the soil?

God, what do you know, that I don't yet know, about this next season?

An Important Note about Days 6 and 7: Communion and Rest

This is one of the most basic rhythms of our life. What God sets in motion on Days 1–5 is still in motion. It's easy to discern and doesn't require a master's in theology or even the ability to read to feel, experience, and appreciate. It's written all over the natural world, the context of our lives. Days 6 and 7 are a little bit different because it's where humans enter the story. Notice that the movements of our lives are one) to move with God ala Adam and Eve where power looks like stewarding creation from the built-in connection of communion (bless, multiply, fill together—not dominate, trash, or destroy). And 2) Rest, the pinnacle day of creation—a space of play and proper alignment: God is God, humans are humans and don't need to try to be God.

This pattern is built into our twenty-four-hour rhythms. It's built into our week and in the Hebrew culture through weekly Shabbat. It's built into much of the Hebrew calendar. The land gets seasons to rest, debt is put to rest every so often, and the entire community stops to rest from work and celebrate the abundance of the harvest. Many of these rhythms and rights of passage are all but lost to much of the Western world. This puts us at a disadvantage when it comes to the practice of "move in communion and rest, move in communion and rest." For many of us, this is a foreign concept.

Notice what happens when you hold your schedule up into the light. What happens when you ask for healthy separations to take place in your schedule, the kind that brings beauty and distinction and boundaries that protect all for the sake of actual connection? Notice what happens when we get the perspective of the stars and the built-in rhythms of the season on our yearly schedules and the ways we choose to spend our days.

What would happen if we saw our calendar through the lens of abundance rather than the hiding place of lack? These questions are worth doing practice on. Picture it in your mind. Ask good questions of yourself and God and note what comes to mind after you ask them. Get into action from a place of true mindfulness—the kind that sees your mind as full and brimming with the kind of thoughts that can be transformed into gold through good questions, curiosity, and self-discovery.

Here's another way to look at rest: all of life is the discovery of what is, and what is, is that we are one. What that means is life-giving rest forever.

SECTION THREE—
OUT OF THE BOX TOOL

Before you begin using the Out of the Box tool, you may want to continue on and read the supplemental thoughts on Hearing God's voice, then come back and practice the tool.

We've discussed the limitation of the boxes we place on ourselves but how do we get out of our mental strongholds? I'm not talking about a thought or two that is limiting but whole structures of well-managed limitations that we have bought into for much of our life? How do we break them down without breaking down, and how do we even see what they are? It's easier than you'd think, especially now that you know how alchemic your thinking can be. It just takes a practice of thought that leads you out. I created this tool because one morning I woke up from a dream and it was a crystal clear train of thought that I woke up into. It was so clear that I knew I needed to write it down before it melted away.

Remember, a box is anything that keeps you limited. Caged. Restrained. Restricted. Held up. Held back. Stuck. Obligated. It drains life from you and brings both confusion and a false sense of clarity. Boxes often tell us two differing stories. I sat with a friend who needed to get unstuck.

Here's what her box told her about her marriage:

- You should trust.
- You should stay.
- You must never leave.
- You must protect yourself and your kids.
- You should never trust.
- You shouldn't stay.
- You should leave.
- You can never protect yourself or your kids.

She was seeking to hear God's voice and find her own. The great thing about doing the box tool is that we were able to let those shoulds and shouldn'ts, as contradictory as they were, come to the surface. One thing was clear: those statements above were not God nor were they her voice. They were simply the walls of the box that was causing her to feel completely torn and confused.

Sometimes we feel held hostage—that's a box. Sometimes we feel a nagging sense that there's just something more—probably a box keeping the "something more" at bay.

There's likely a "false self" box that has been a safe place and refuge for you but will continue keeping you from enjoying your authentic self much less sharing it or living from it without apology.

How do you know if and where there are boxes keeping you from soaring?

- Low-level under-the-surface dissatisfaction.
- Inability to fully express yourself, your ideas, your dreams—feeling held back.
- Little to no free-flowing creativity in a particular area.
- The sense that there's more.
- An inability to make a choice.
- Feeling like a victim.

- Shoulds, woulds, and coulds that seem to sit between you and your fuller and fullest life.
- Clear "Can't evers"—"will nevers" or "musts" that drive your ship (your life is one big vow).
- Depression.
- Numbness.
- Feeling cornered and squelched.
- Feeling unknown and like there's no place you really belong.

The worst thing that boxes do is that they keep us isolated. Isolation is deadly. It is perhaps the greatest issue that we as Westerners are experiencing the horrors of. We often don't speak up because some horrors are visibly much worse—the pain of war, the trauma of violence and abuse. But some are so subtle that their impact that the pain is not as easily identified: isolation, shame, judgment, disconnect, disembodiment, self-sabotage, and relational insecurity.

Do you feel isolated at all from your real self? The deepest heart of hearts that God gave you and made you live from will benefit from getting out of a box or two.

Do you feel isolated from people that you used to connect with easily? Maybe you feel largely misunderstood, disappointed, and even fearful of close connection? You will be helped to step out of the confines of whatever cage is keeping you from receiving and giving love freely.

Do you feel isolated from God? You might "believe" but if you were honest, you aren't sure if God exists much less that He is intimately involved in your life. These are the kinds of boxes I most love to see smashed because God has never existed well inside the boxes humans create. This life works best if we live inside the actual world He created rather than creating systems to contain Him/Her/Them (by them I mean God the Father and Mother, God the Holy Spirit, and God's Kids ala Jesus—as *one*).

Like the viscosity of the great Amazon River, strong enough to support a division of water lines—a two-in-one river, separate yet intermingling. You are a river, made to uniquely flow in the "confines" of all the other great rivers, together as one and yet distinct, with your own flow, flavor, colors, and strengths.

You are a river. It's time to flow.

Ready? Let's go! Use one of the following box templates. The first is more simple than the second. If you choose the first, ignore the instructions about arrows in the text below and simply write your shoulds/oughts/musts/would-if-I-coulds inside the box, then write your new statements outside the box starting at the top as a letter to yourself, line by line. The 3rd image is an example of what a partially filled in box might look like.

SHOULD/SHOULDN'T	OUGHT/OUGHT NOT
MUST/CAN NEVER	WOULD IF I COULD

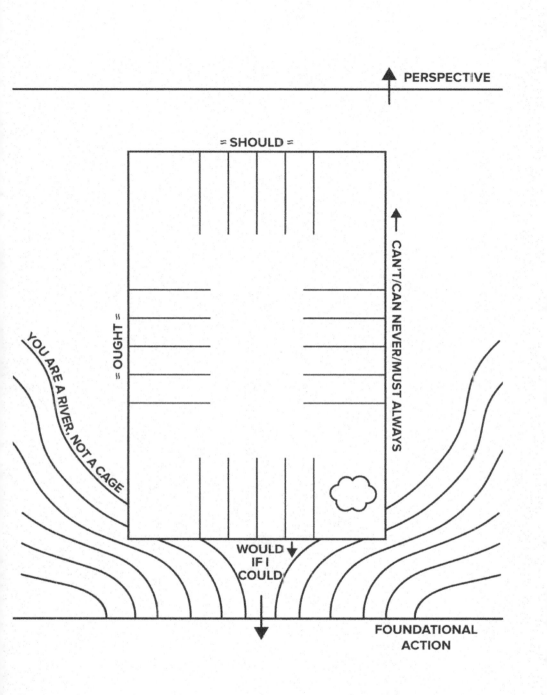

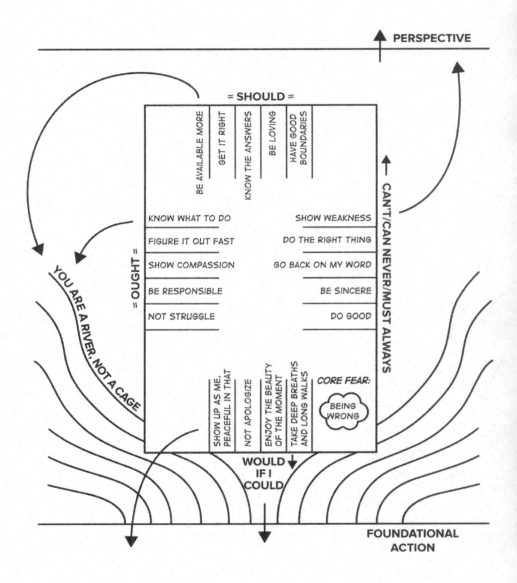

PERSPECTIVE

= SHOULD =

BE AVAILABLE MORE
GET IT RIGHT
KNOW THE ANSWERS
BE LOVING
HAVE GOOD BOUNDARIES

= OUGHT =

KNOW WHAT TO DO
FIGURE IT OUT FAST
SHOW COMPASSION
BE RESPONSIBLE
NOT STRUGGLE

SHOW WEAKNESS
DO THE RIGHT THING
GO BACK ON MY WORD
BE SINCERE
DO GOOD

CAN'T/CAN NEVER/MUST ALWAYS

YOU ARE A RIVER, NOT A CAGE

SHOW UP AS ME, PEACEFUL IN THAT
NOT APOLOGIZE
ENJOY THE BEAUTY OF THE MOMENT
TAKE DEEP BREATHS AND LONG WALKS

CORE FEAR:
BEING WRONG

WOULD
IF I
COULD

FOUNDATIONAL
ACTION

There are a couple ways to go at this.

1. You can use this simply as a tool to further your own thinking.

2. You can use this to have a conversation with God.

Both are beneficial and you can try it both ways. Sometimes it's hard to separate the two and that's normal.

When people ask God about their boxes, this normally leads to breakthroughs because God carries a level of knowledge about you and your boxes that you are not yet aware of but you have full access to through mental dialogue.

I am happy to walk you through this either way; if you prefer way 1. you will simply ask yourself the questions that follow.

If you prefer way 2. go ahead and skip down to Section B.

Some of you may find it interesting to do this from a place of personal reflection (1.) then do it again from a place of asking God about it (2.) and note the differences.

Personal Processing Tool: Box Awareness (1.)

1. What situation or mindset do you want to get out of the box of? You may just want to go through this as a generic "get out of *your* box"—meaning the way you see the world and act in it daily.

    Pick one and write it in the middle of the box - it could just be your name or it could be a situation you find yourself in.

2. Ask yourself what your "Shoulds" are around the central situation/ mindset or generic personal box you are examining. For example,

if in the middle of my page, I put "Cayce," then I'm gonna brainstorm about general "shoulds" that I feel in my life, such as:

- I should listen well to people.

- I should appease my family.

- I should not push anyone on anything, especially not my ideas.

- I should not go too far in front of anyone in thinking so they don't feel left out.

You get the idea. Roll with what comes up that seems like the way that you think about life in regards to "shoulds." It will be different for everyone. By nature of a should, it's not necessarily the freest version of yourself; it comes from the story you tell yourself from a place of less than, guilt or shame but you're probably unaware of how subtle it is. It comes from your personal experiences and the story you've told yourself about them in order to make sense of the world. Don't put what you think the answer "should be." Take the time to fetter out the way you actually function. What are the "should rules" that guide your actions? Some of these things could be "true" (such as: of course, it's good to listen well to people) but this isn't about what is true or false and good or bad. This is about getting unstuck from what limits us or what motivates us from shame rather than freedom. This exercise will help you shift from being motivated by "I really should" to a place of choice that sounds more like: "I want to do this," which is a very different place for thoughts to live and manifest in our lives.

Write each should or shouldn't statement/thought you come up with (write small!) in the box under the word "Should."

3. Do the exact same thing but using the prompt: "Oughts." This sounds a lot like the "Shoulds" but it's not quite the same; it's stronger, and it's a sense of what you really just ought to do in order to be right (in your own eyes/culture/upbringing/experience).

List these in the box near the word "Oughts."

4. Now move to the part of the box that says "Can't/Must Always"

What do you feel that you "Must always or never do" think/say/feel/be?

List these in that part of the box. Trust what comes to mind even if it feels very subtle.

5. What do you feel that you "Can't" or "Can never do" think/say/feel/be? What have you vowed that you simply won't do? What have you vowed or promised that keeps you loyal to a certain action or perception? This is where you look at things you've always said or stood by that function like a law to you. Take a minute here and look at whether or not there is an emotion or motivation that you can see driving this whole side of the box. If so, put that at the bottom of this side.

Write these inside the box beside "Always will, must never."

6. Do the same thing for the prompt: "What would I do *if I could*?"

If there was nothing in the way, no rules and no "way things should be," what would you do?

Write these in the box "Would if I could" section.

Great Job! Now let's begin moving out of our boxes.

1. Look at your "Shoulds" line by line.

   For every single "should" that's in the box, you will write a new thought outside the box line by line like a letter. (For the 2nd template, use the flowy river-looking lines).

   Imagine yourself holding the statements loosely and being willing to look at them from a broader perspective - imagine zooming out and stepping back from these statements. Make sure the new thought is more loving, gracious, and spacious. If it's a thought that feels freer and as if there is more than one choice, it will be a helpful perspective to consider. Let the new thought that you write out of the box serve as a counter statement to the first confining statement.

   *If you struggle to come up with a counter statement or think that what is in your box simply "is the way things are" do one of two things: star the statement in the box as a way of reminding yourself to revisit it later or you may want to jump to Section 2. for help from an outside Source, hearing God's voice can really help.

2. When you are finished with your "Shoulds," do the same for the "Oughts."

   Write them out of the box (on the flowing lines if using template 2).

3. *Next write counter-statements for your "Can't, won't, must never, and always will" side of the box. Template 1, write out of the box. Template 2, write your statements at the top in the "Perspective" section.*

   Take each sentence and rewrite your own narrative here. It may require you to intentionally have grace on yourself and others. Remember here that forgiveness of self, others, life and God always moves us out of vows and is an essential human practice in order to release stuck narratives and mindsets.

If you hold yourself or others in judgment, these vows will function like compulsions for you. What is helpful is to see beyond them.

4. Look at your statements near "I would if I could." Ask yourself genuinely, *"what if I could?"*

Take a minute to let your own heart speak to you about what is possible together, from an integrated place. What do I mean by integrated? I mean that place where the core of you aligns with the exterior of you. Where your desires are given space to move and where the inner voice is honored. The space where your dreams, desires, wants, and visions are not immediately squashed by "reason" or life, but instead, they are honored as vital. If you haven't ever honored this space of conversation within yourself as vital to all you do, take a minute to apologize to yourself. Then treat yourself the way you'd want your child, favorite person, or the best person you know to be treated. Try going further than you normally do in listening to your own self/heart/desires.

Write your new statements out of the box for template 1 or for template 2 at the bottom of the page under "Foundational Action."

5. Finally, ask yourself what feeling or word holds you inside the box? What are you afraid of?

Write it in the box (use the cloud on template 2.) and then ask yourself for a new word to replace that fear and write it out of the box. Take a minute to breathe the fear/negative word out, releasing your heart, mind and body from it. Breathe in the new word and receive it like a gift.

Great! You have done your first Out of the Box exercise.

Once you gain awareness of what the box rules were, they can be just that: box rules. They do not need to define your life. Now you have a choice. You can act according to the box but before you do, ask what it costs you and what it feels like for you. Now make a choice remembering you can always adjust now that you are aware of the thoughts driving your action.

Try out the lifestyle of the river waters that you just created. Put them before your eyes tonight before you go to bed. Wake up and engage them. Make intentional choices tomorrow because of them and see what happens. What do you notice? Do some of the "in-the-box statements" seem slightly ridiculous yet? What can you get started on today from the foundational action statements at the bottom of your page?

Now for processing the box from a place of listening to that deep internal voice of Spirit, God's voice.

I'll lead you through a similar version to what you see above. You may notice that while God speaks in a voice that sounds like the way you think, what is said will be deeper and wiser than your norm because accessing God's voice is accessing the collective wisdom of the universe. It's endlessly deep and wide, sometimes silent (in a peaceful way), but never harmful.

Let's go!

Connecting with God's Voice Processing Tool: Out of the Box (2.)

1. *Ask Jesus/God: What scenario would it benefit to do this "out of the box" on?* If what comes to mind is your own name, that will work. It may be a situation or even another person's perspective. Whatever the case, understand that it's a false or boxed-in version of yourself, other's or the situation.

   Write what comes to mind in the middle of the page.

2. Ask Jesus/God: What "Shoulds/shouldn'ts" do I hold about this topic? (If it's you, say "What are my shoulds/shouldn'ts?")

   Write each thing that pops into your mind (write small!) in the box by the word "Shoulds."

3. Now you'll do the exact same thing but ask God about your "Oughts." This sounds a lot like the "Shoulds" but it's not. It's stronger and comes with a strong sense of what you really just ought to do.

   List these in the box next to "Oughts."

4. There are 3 parts to this one

   • Ask: Jesus/God, what do I feel that I must always do/think/say/feel/be?

   List anything that pops in your mind in the "Must always/always will/always should/ought" category.

   • Ask: Jesus/God, what do I feel that I never can do/think/say/feel/be?

   List anything that pops in your mind.

- Ask: Jesus/God, what have I promised myself/vowed that I simply won't ever or always will do?

List what comes to mind.

5. Now look at the bottom of the box and ask God: "What would I do *if I could*?" If there was nothing in the way and no rules and no "way things should be," what would I do?

Write these in the box near the "Would if I could" section.

Great Job! Now let's move out of the box.

1. Look at your "Shoulds" line by line.

   For every single "should" that's in the box, you will ask God what is real and write that starting at the top as a letter to yourself for template 1 or on the river-looking lines if using template 2. As you list these things on the flowing lines, continue to write small because your "Oughts" will go here too.

   Example: Jesus, a should I've held is that I always care for others. What is real (or true) from your heart to mine? (Record what comes first.) "Cayce, you do care for others but I never intended for that to be at the expense of your own self-care. I'll show you how to care for yourself and those I've put in your life in a healthy way."

   What's in the quotes is what I would put in my letter out of the box or on the river/flowing lines.

2. When you finish your "Shoulds," do the same for the "Oughts."

3. Now move to the "Can't/must never/must always" side of the box.

Listen to God about each statement and add to your letter outside of the box or write what comes to mind at the top of the page in the section that says "Perspective" on template 2.

*Remember that forgiveness of self, others, and God always frees us from unspoken and spoken vows. Forgiveness is an essential human health practice that is for your benefit. Otherwise, vows can function like compulsions in your life.

4. Now listen to God about your "would if I could" section.

    Write what comes to mind as you ask God outside of the box adding to your letter. If you are using template 2 put it at the bottom under "Foundational action."

    *Remember to check what you think you might be hearing from God. Does it sound loving and life-giving? Does it bring peace and wisdom to you? Is it free of judgment and condemnation? What do you feel as you think about the words coming to mind? Be honest and stay in the conversation with God.

Great job! If you need rest after doing this, notice that and give yourself the care you need.

It's tiring to hold on to limiting mindsets. Often when we realize we don't have to anymore, our body and mind will want a break to reset - this is the kind of rest that is very productive and healing so don't cheat yourself out of it. It's well deserved and much needed; honor how you are feeling and get some good rest as needed. You might need movement now instead of rest, notice what your heart, mind and body feel and need.

Examples of Boxes from My Life

God has graciously been pulling us out of our identity boxes, our mindsets, and our experience gaps since day one.

I imagine I've been a fun case.

I'm pretty sure, as lovely as I was in my infancy, I didn't want to leave the warm dark cove of the womb. In fact, I'm quite sure I was terrified. Yet out I finally tumbled, forceps were deemed necessary and I have a crooked smile to prove it. Out of the box.

Pervasive fear tagged along into childhood. I assumed it was the cage I was made for, at best. Even worse, I assumed that fear was simply a part of me.

At six, I experienced the first miracle of my life (that I was aware of). Fear dreams plagued my nights. My interpretation of these dreams was that: a) I was bad; b) I could never tell anyone; c) I was in danger; d) I couldn't escape; e) I might as well make friends with fear because I was trapped.

The limiting believe that I could never tell anyone was me trying to protect myself, but it was limiting just like the other understandable interpretations I made. It kept me silent about the dream's content. (Now I'm glad to give you the short version to spare you the traumatic details. In the dream I was being kidnapped, strategically dismembered and sliced to pieces. Nice.)

My mom helped me out of this early, very physically and emotionally exhausting cage of a dream that was too much for my six-year-old self to handle.

One night she came in at bedtime. Knowing I had been having terrifying dreams but not knowing what they were, she said, "Cayce, we're just going to ask Jesus to take these dreams away tonight, and we're going to pray that you never, ever have another one."

This was the first time I remember God outright intervening in my life.

I never had that dream again even though I remember it to this day. In fact, I've never really had a "bad" dream again. I've had beautiful dreams, odd dreams, and processing dreams that surface insecurities and fears. I've had dreams that act like warnings to me but I have never ever been terrified by a dream again.

Today, I value the way God communicates through dreams at night as much as I value communication and experiences of God's presence in the day. I'm so grateful to be out of the bad-dream box.

Dream terrors no longer existed but a constant low level of anxiety and fear certainly remained.

Signs were easy to spot if anyone was paying much attention: constant stomach aches, labeled "shy" all too often, days riddled with anxiety, nightly recurring fear of the darkness, "She's a little bit sensitive" my mom wrote in my first-grade notes to the teacher. Sensitive? Everything was terrifying. New haircut? Terrible. New friends? Butterflies for days. Carnival rides? Hell no. Push me out of my comfort zone. No. No. And No.

My mind was plagued with what could and probably would at some point go terribly wrong.

If I speak, I'll be heard and seen—nope.

If I get on that ride, the rollercoaster will run off track and leave me crushed bleeding out—nope.

If I don't measure up to all the "expectations" that I carefully spent time discerning (also making up) that everyone had of me, especially those in authority but really anyone—then all will be lost. I'll be hated forever and I might as well die. Nope.

Sounds extreme, I know.

Let's pause here and recognize that the last paragraph is one of my big, personal life rule "boxes" that I didn't discover until my late thirties.

Consciously, I didn't walk around afraid I would die (at least not all the time). Subconsciously this fear hovered just under the surface driving me to cling to the cage that I was carefully fashioning around my heart, my life, my friends, my family, my faith, my city, and my world so that I and everyone else could simply survive.

It's taken a good thirty-five years of prayer, experiences, people, conversation, and risk to see the cage more fully for the not-oh-so-wonderful but seemingly "essential" place that I have spent much of my life.

Here are some facts about cages: they are usually small; they seem smaller the more we grow; if not exited they will actually stunt and restrict growth; they are limiting in almost every way but, yes, they are originally protective and created so we can survive.

While a cage does limit movement and freedom, even more so, it limits things like joy (the kind that shows on the outside), creativity, and hope—the real stuff, not wishful thinking but a life full of eager expectation of what's next because it's gonna be good!

Limited thinking shoots hope in the foot everytime making it seem like small, pithy, positive statements of affirmation.

This is really a shame because *hope* is designed to function like a tree of life for us bringing our desires to fruition.

When we are in a cage, we are simply afraid to think much about hope. This is an honest reaction to the cage because who could engage a life of embodied hope in a cage?

In the cage, we may whisper dreams but we will rarely embody them. Nonetheless, the whispering is important. It's a quiet, but embodied action that serves as one toe in the river of life where you'll find your personal flow and freedom. Hope is what moves us into the river more and more fully.

Maybe your whisper is the first step toward a vision of a world beyond what you now see. Whispered dreams are a prayer for a type of world other than the cages we've crafted.

A final fact about cages: we all have them, use them, love them, and then ultimately hate them. They function on a spectrum between protection and self-sabotage. Moving out of them from a place of connection to God is a safe way of being for your heart, mind and body. Moving out of these boxes will integrate your heart, mind and body bringing an inner integrity that impacts everything external in your life.

It's the way of humanity, at least initially, to cling to structures, even invisibly crafted personal structures, to help us feel safe. At first, they seem like a suitable place to be ourselves.

The problem is this: they will always ultimately restrict us from full expression.

I was the kind of kid who liked the idea of reading but didn't really read that much. I was book smart so I always did what I needed to do but I was afraid of both breaking the rules and expending too much energy (remember, according to my personal survival rules I was trying to find the delicate balance between living right and not dying). So my happy medium was to be a stellar grade getter and tops on the list of the teachers' "most obedient and self-controlled" list (you're welcome teachers) but not a true learner because I'd stand out and get too much attention which felt like exposure and that was a big trigger for me.

"Learners" risk needing to get everything right in order to actually dive in and tinker on a subject. Learners immerse themselves in a topic just for fun, they are willing to get it wrong and fail out of pure interest. Blowing a quiz because I was too busy exploring the intricacies of one specific topic that stole my imagination and curiosity? That was never me but learners do that kind of thing all the time.

I read a few books outside of what was assigned. Too much energy, I might get distracted and miss my teacher's directions on how exactly to center my name on the line at the left of the page the next day and then I'd have to: a) get up out of my seat and ask for a repeat of the directions, proving my inability to pay attention (gasp!) Or b) potentially put myself in a position of getting something terribly wrong with my spacing and risk being chastised personally or, horror of horrors, corrected in front of the class.

I was a very normal kid, not neurotic at all (note the sarcasm). Just like you.

This is my life box on full display. Yours may not look like mine, but I promise, you've got boxes too: for yourself, for your life, for your work, for your family, and for your future. They give the illusion of control and as humans, we share a deep fondness for them.

I can only remember one book that I really enjoyed reading outside of class. I read it three or four times. *They Cage the Animals at Night* by Jennings Michael Burch. It was the first "adult" leisure (not really, it's a tough book to read. I originally typed pleasure, but it's not that kind of book either) book I'd ever picked up.

The subtitle of the book is *The True Story of an Abandoned Child's Struggle for Emotional Survival*. Que: insight into Cayce's issues and life trajectory.

Some of my interest in this book must have come out of my own anxiety about what kind of horrors could happen to me (and preparing to survive them).

Some of my interest certainly came out of micro-horrors that had happened to me.

Another part of my interest in this particular book was simply about the bent that my life would lean toward: healing. Healing because I needed it. Healing because others needed it. Healing because no one comes out of life without bruises. Freedom: does it exist? What is it? How does it function? Is it safe? Can people recover from trauma? These have been fascinating and fabulous topics to spend my life on.

A Few Thoughts on Wounds—
WE'VE ALL GOT THEM!

Just like physical bruises and wounds, life wounds show up after hurtful experiences to indicate that something hurt us. They tell us that some form of trauma has impacted us. While shame often causes us to try to hide and cover our emotional and spiritual wounding, our wounds are nothing to stay ashamed of.

Traumas happen emotionally, spiritually, and physically. They indicate places where healing is needed and where healing is also *happening*. Did you know that post-traumatic stress, as painful and debilitating as it can be, when measured next to the coexisting post-traumatic growth in an individual pales by comparison? Yes, trauma is very difficult and the processing of pain is valid. It's encouraging to see that it is usually outpaced by the growth also taking place in our lives. *They coexist but often we are most aware of the pain.* The ultimate growth that comes from trauma often totally eclipses trauma's pain, especially when people are given safe spaces to feel what they feel and process it without judgment or invalidation.

Where you find trauma, you will also find healing and growth. It's not one or the other. It's both beauty and ashes. The growth may be ignored, unacknowledged, unmeasured, or seemingly disconnected from the trauma but that does not mean it's not there.

You could say that our bumps, bruises, and imperfections "speak" or indicate that something happened. They are inextricably linked to our stories and our strengths. This is redemptive but it doesn't always mean it's easy to navigate or that the path is clear.

Wounds show up in our lives to tell us our own stories and to invite us to acknowledge both the growth we've experienced and the healing we need.

Pain and trauma triggers tell us to slow down and let our bodies and souls do what they are made to do: heal.

Healing and growth are rivers that flow physically throughout our bodies at a supernatural pace doing all kinds of supernatural and beneficial things. This is a scientific fact. It's happening in your veins as we speak, enabling you to read this book without worrying about much else, unless you'd like to worry about other things. Then you can, but your body will keep pumping that blood at just the right temperature through your precious, far-reaching circulatory system.

Everything about your physical, emotional, spiritual self wants to flow because it was made to flow. Flow enables us to function more freely with fewer limitations. Wounds are not who we are. They indicate we need healing so we can return to the full functioning of who we are—body, soul, and spirit as one—or however it makes sense to you to divide that up and integrate it back together. We know that these parts of ourselves are deeply interconnected. The words just help us understand. They don't really mean that they are separate. You are one beautiful being made to flow, growing in your awareness of how connected you are from the inside out.

Sometimes it helps to look at life's traumas and wounds through the lens of the boxes that they have shaped for us to live in long after the actual bruising heals and fades away.

A friend of mine defines trauma as anything we experience that we cannot fully understand. I love this because it's easy to see that we all experience some form of trauma quite often. When we don't understand what we experience, we jump past the processing and begin constructing boxes to make sure that we are prepared to survive the next time we are taken by surprise.

Everyone does this often; it's human. Not only is it normal but it's psychologically helpful at times. Beginning to recognize how a box functions brings us to the awareness we need to choose something else when we are ready to move on. At this point, we can evaluate if the box is doing much good anymore.

When I was ten, I visited my Aunt Pat in Amarillo, Texas. She had recently moved and I played in the cardboard moving boxes in her driveway for hours after she unpacked her new home. Her neighbor's son and I became fast friends helping each other hide in a box and then burst out. We cut holes in them and taped them together to form tunnels and forts. I want that for you. You may not be ready to bust out of old boxes that gave you a sense of security just yet, but perhaps you could playfully navigate the boxes in your life. If you can take the old walls and playfully build new and fun spaces for your life, then that is a fabulous use of your creative energy. It's far better than patching old cardboard to cover your wounds. Coming out of hiding is a key part of our growth and development; recognizing that we're hiding in the first place is the first step.

Since we all create boxes and often get lost in their habitat, let's not waste time in shame or wringing our hands about it. Let's learn to navigate them freely.

It is not necessary for the purposes of this book to delve deep into personal healing to get out of your boxes. Having said that, seek healing as you need it! See a counselor! Get inner healing! Everyone needs it, and if you are interested in living out of the box, I am going to assume you're into growth. So, if you have a box that tells you you can't ask for help or it's a selfish waste of time to get healing, that you can't have needs or admit imperfection, get out of that box so you can grow and flow!

I bring up wounds not to deal with them here but to make the point that we all have them and they have undoubtedly shaped our lives. Let them create your strength and presence to life rather than inhibit or hide you.

While this book isn't directly about healing, anyone can sign up for a virtual connection appointment at ONE, where I work. Our team has decades of experience helping people heal and grow under their belt! If you've read this book and still aren't sure how to connect with the voice of God that's already available to you, our team can help. It won't hurt!

You can find us at www.theonejourney.com

From big boxes to the small easily crushed boxes, if it holds you or your dreams inside, it's time for them to go.

This little book may hold the keys to the most empowering tool you ever learn—not just how to discern boxes but how to get out of them.

The book I mentioned that I was so drawn to as a kid, *They Cage the Animals at Night,* is a true story about an eight year old left at the steps of an orphanage. In the story, Michael has only one constant in his life: his stuffed animal, "Doggie." He has lost his parents and every shred of belonging he had ever known, so Doggie embodies belonging to Michael like nothing else. In his new orphanage, all the kids' stuffed animals are locked away at night. It's a heart-wrenching story. Beloved Doggie. Constant companion. The only one who has shared Michael's entire journey. The one who loves unconditionally. The one who embodied hope for Michael: locked up.

Looking at our own boxes is like taking the key to the cage holding Michael's Doggie and unlocking an old friend. Your boxes have kept you safe but they have also locked up something of great *value and belonging* inside. The fact that the box exists tells us there is hope. Authentic human belonging, comfort, and connection are counterintuitively found inside of those old locked boxes. Hope is hidden, even protected, there.

Unveiling, unearthing, and unlocking the parts of yourself that have been boxed in will always be steps in the journey to your real self, your true home— the only fitting shelter for you.

SUPPLEMENTAL THOUGHTS ON HEARING GOD'S VOICE

Why you can…

First, let's start with a quick lesson on how to hear the always-available, still-small voice of God. Does God speak in many other ways? Of course! But the most consistent is through what has been created. The piece of creation that you know inside out is your own body. So your mind is the place where you will be most attuned to the still-small voice and where you will find it.

Your ability to hear God is not determined by your experience, the strength of your belief, your Bible knowledge, your church history, or your best intentions. You cannot stop God's voice in your life, so you might as well learn to tune in.

Your ability to hear God is 100 percent determined by who you are as the "Created" and breathed-upon species (humans). You were *designed* to hear God. (Unless God didn't make you, then you're not—*just kidding*!) Whether you know it or not, you were made by a God who made you hear His/Her voice because He/She is kind, involved, smart, and capable of incredible depth in relationships.

God's boundless capacity for all things means you too are capable of connection with God by virtue of your status as a created, loved being. You did not choose this. Can a piece of art say to its maker, "You didn't make me!"? Well if it could talk, it sure could say that, think that, and even feel that, but it doesn't change what's real: its artist. The painting was painted by the artist who created it. Period.

If the artist loved the painting yet the painting hated itself (very impressive painting to feel this deeply and communicate like this), does the artwork's personal interpretation change the perspective of the artist? Not likely. You know artists; they have their opinions.

If one of my five kids decided they were no longer a member of the Harris family, or if they moved to the other side of the earth and changed their name, does it change the fact that they are our child? Just ask this momma who birthed these five children naturally in birthing pools if they are mine! Nothing that my kids could ever do, think, change, or feel can undo the fact that they came from me and I adore them. Whether they like it, believe it, share it, or care about it, they are my kids through and through forever. Period.

What if the God who put us into families (as messy as that can be) is no different? Our Source, whether we feel it/believe it/like it/understand it, simply is. Except for one difference: this Source is a Source to all that is truly good, lovely, generative, life-giving, light-bearing, and creative. The family DNA has been deposited in us. These are seeds of freedom, joy, hope, wisdom, life, love, nurture, creativity, purpose, help, protection, authenticity, and grace. I could go on, but you get the picture. These are the things that often threaten us that we discussed in Section 2. It's far more threatening to our boxes to think that we are empowered. It's easier to hide behind fear, pain, and shame than to move into self-possession and expression. But at some point, it must be done because the life in you just has to grow. The boxes will actually make sure of it. Understanding this will allow you to embrace the entire journey, releasing your judgment of the past, the pain, the boxes, yourself, others, the world, and God.

My favorite picture of this is from the Original Garden—two trees.

One: "of life." Those are two little words that say and mean so much. OF LIFE. That's it. If life's not part of it, the fruit didn't come from this tree.

The other: "of the knowledge of good and evil." And darn if this isn't the perfect picture for what we all pick. To know about good and evil, to understand, to draw lines about which is which, to make judgments, to do the boundary setting and approval seeking and striving, that is simply too much for a mere mortal to bear well.

God constantly, throughout the story of mankind has been offering life from the center of His good and beautiful garden. The hungry, the hurt, the questioning, the lonely, the humble, the ashamed, the fearful, the too-strong, the too-far outs, the not-welcome-here, the oppressed, and the downtrodden, they can all show you the path to the "of life" tree that tells a better story than the "knowledge" tree. Many religious paths create spiritual experiences in life. But where religion operates without the power of life as the central experience, often we are left with nothing to do but dictate what is right and what is wrong and judge ourselves, others, and life according to it. This will never lead to life even if the words sound really good.

What does God sound like?

Take the "of life" understanding and apply it broadly. A look at the story of God and God's people throughout six thousand years of handed-down stories—the Bible—is an important place to start. Don't pull out one verse about slavery or homosexuality to make a point. That's the most horrific way you could ever use someone's story—to oppress and justify the oppression of another life. No, don't pull one verse that suits you from a culture and time period way before you. Instead, look at the trajectory of the whole story. What's the overarch?

Here are a few for reference as you listen to God and have your own dia-logue-rich conversation.

- Redemption. Restoring all the broken pieces, putting things and people back together

- Life. The kind that feeds and nourishes the body, soul, and spirit of all humankind.

- Peace. The kind that passes by our comprehension and understanding.

- Creativity. Good ideas, beauty, reproduction, and re-creation.

- Anger. The authentic anger of God is always and only focused on the things that break us, steal from us, and deceive us. God exhib-its anger but it's not at you. It's for you. Always. And not because you're good (because you did the right thing) but because God's good and so are God's image bearers—anyone breathing, whether we live that out or not. What happens to us long before we have cognition, language, and mature choice directly impacts whether our choices reflect the image of God, but the potential is there and never void of possibility.

- Provision. All the provision needed for our flourishing and pro-tection is found in God.

- Conviction. It's the kindness of God that leads us to change our ways and to change the way we think. The hallmark of conviction is that with it comes freedom. God's correction feels good and leads to good for us. It has no judgment in it at all.

- Grace. There's simply no judgment toward you in God, only judg-ment toward what harms you, the Beloved. So you can stop wor-rying and just be loved. It's who you are.

- Wisdom. The wisdom of the ages is nothing compared to the wisdom at hand in conversation with God. Connection to God causes wisdom to flow naturally to you and through you.

There are more, but you get the idea.

What God doesn't sound like (other voices):

What does God *not* sound like (please take the idea of God speaking/sounding and apply it broadly: look, feel, seem, act like—God's ways)?

Though God speaks through people, it's rare that one person always sounds like God, even if they claim to speak on God's behalf. My kids often misquote me, misunderstand me, and generally get it wrong. This is a normal phenomenon with children. They are growing and learning. Most importantly, we are growing in the relationship. I don't care whether they quote me right; I care that they continue to know my heart and grow in their own beautiful expressions of their hearts in a way that blesses them, blesses others, and blesses the world. I'm not the best mom, but I think I get God a little bit here, and God is truly the much better parent!

Tactics God doesn't use, so when you "hear" or "think" thoughts that seem to come from these places, you can let them go and think again with God. He simply cannot speak from these places because God is not these things:

- Fear. God not only tells us not to use this hundreds of times throughout the course of the Bible but because God is radical and full of love, fear doesn't have any place to operate when it comes to God's intentions and motivations. So if you think a thought that sounds fear-driven or fearful, it's not God. Does God warn and protect like any good protector/provider would? Yes, but a voice of fear that incites fear simply cannot be from God.

- Shame. God is the One who called to Adam and Eve in the garden to come out of hiding. They were not told to hide themselves. They did so naturally when they fed on what was not life. God, in great grace, made clothes for them, not to hide them but to help them move out of the paralyzing ashamed state they were feeling. God doesn't shame us or use shame to tame us. It's something else talking to you if it sounds like shame.

- Manipulation (guilting). God isn't just into getting God's way so the His/Her version of control isn't at all like the petty manipulation or control that we use that is ultimately a myth. God moves with good intentions, not to produce an outcome but to see us grow and be free. In fact, God, who controls everything, chose to give away "control" by giving us free choice. This is something only the most secure and unmanipulative of beings would do. God's not trying to put the chess pieces on a board so that you are forced into anything. God doesn't speak in a way that brings about a physical result detached from the heart—only manipulation does that and it's ugly. It can be hard to see, so ask God to show you what it is and what it sounds like so that you are not moved by it or choose to use it.

- Condemnation. There's a big difference between condemnation and conviction. Condemnation often feels like a box built by control, shame, or guilt rather than freedom. It speaks negatively to our *identity* as bad rather than simply helping us see that our *choice* was bad. Conviction helps us see another way for what it is: *life*. Condemnation reiterates that we are bad and cannot get it right because of how bad we are. Those are called lies.

- Hostility. As mentioned earlier, God gets angry all right but it will never be taken out on you; it's for you. It's like the roar of a lion over her cubs. It's about your protection and healing, and it's not directed at you.

- Form of religion apart from the connection (shoulds, oughts). God doesn't direct apart from loving connection. So if you are "hearing" a ton of shoulds/oughts and "you better ____ or you need to" ____ and it doesn't sound relieving (peaceful, free, encouraging), it's probably a form of godliness (words that sound like God, but it's not God) without the actual power of God (God's Presence Itself). I see this as the best example of what is meant by "You shall not take the name of Yahweh, Your God, in vain."[5] When we use Jesus' name to legitimize something God is not actually saying—maybe it's fear-based, shame-based, control-seeking, or violent (harmful to God's loved ones) in nature, then we are using God's name in a very vain way and this does much damage. Likewise, when you seek to hear God's voice—when you notice a thought that comes to you that might "sound like" what you think God would say, but it doesn't have freedom, peace, and life in it, check to make sure it's not just a vain version of religion talking. If it is, take it to Jesus and ask for His actual thoughts. They will flow quickly once you ask.

These two charts are helpful and simple:

---

5.   Exodus 20:7 (ESV).

God's voice

LOVE

LIFE

ABUNDANCE

CONVICTION

KINDNESS (LEADS
TO REPENTANCE)

BELONGING

GRACE/MERCY

CONNECTION

PURPOSE

WISDOM

FREEDOM

RECONCILIATION

HOPE

YOUR VOICE AND CHOICE

Other voices

FEAR

JUDGMENT

LACK

CONDEMNATION

SHAME

STEAL, KILL, DESTROY

ACCUSATION

CONTROL

DISCONNECT

PARANOIA

INSECURITY

OUGHT/SHOULD

DIVISION/SIDES

Artist

CREATION

IMAGE OF GOD

EXPERIENCE

CURIOSITY

CONNECTION

MYSTERY

BELONGING

Accuser/Critic

TEAR DOWN/BUILD UP

GOOD/BAD

RIGHT/WRONG

SHOULD/OUGHT

STUPID/SMART

CERTAINTY/DOUBT

IN/OUT

These are other helpful things to think about when it comes to hearing God:

1. A simple prayer. "Jesus, quiet every voice other than Yours right now." Then go for it. Again, let me emphasize that I use the name Jesus because it's a genuine and true relationship and connection to God for me. I understand that it may not be for you. Do I think that precludes you from a connection with God's voice? No, so use the name you are most comfortable with and that is an honest expression of your voice and thoughts. For me, that's Jesus. For you, it may be "Hey you!"

    It reminds me of the saying by some parents to a child: "I don't care what you call me but just that you do call me." I get that. As a mom, my kids could call me the wrong name and I'd still answer because I just love them and want to talk to them so darn much. I believe this to be a similar situation and I have experienced this to be a similar situation. What do I mean by that? I mean that often I help people who don't know what they think of God or Jesus to have a hearing God session and it works regardless of what they call God. I'll be honest and say that very often, they do engage with Jesus after a while because they want to, not because they had to or I told them to.

2. Know that when you ask God something, God will answer and usually it's fast. Faster than even our cognitive thought speed. For example, as I turn my attention to God's presence in such a way that I'm asking God a question, usually the answer starts to flow to my thoughts/pop into my mind/heart before I even finish the question or very quickly afterward. In general, God is fast and loves to answer us, so His response will come quickly and it's usually the very first thought we think after we ask the question. If this is real and we are tapping into the mind of God with our own minds, expect that to be dynamic, complex in the best way, and fast.

3. God's voice will sound like the way you think. It's not limited by that, but the still small voice will sound like you. It *won't* sound like an old man with a deep gruff voice unless your own inner voice sounds like that. God is *with* us for real and has already been talking to us our whole lives! It sounds very much like our own awesome thoughts. Ever had a great idea? That could have been a God-thought. Ever felt awe? I'm not sure awe arises apart from a connection to a Presence beyond our own. Ever had a pure love for someone and a desire to do them good and not harm? God's voice—apart from this, where does goodness come from? Ever wanted to connect with God, people, and the world around you purely for the sake of relational integrity? That's beautiful! Where do you think that kind of inspiration originates in you?

4. The question is not *if* you can hear God's voice but how to start recognizing that it's really the God-space inside you, that place where you think with God, the mind alchemy space. You already have golden thoughts, but finding the space of connection with God will teach you how to generate them anytime! (Seeing, picturing, thinking, ideating, dreaming—all forms of thought can be taken to a different level of clarity in conversation with the authentic self, God, and others on the journey with you.)

One of my deepest drivers is a desire to be relevant. When I realized this, my first reaction was to judge the word as superficial and flawed. But as I asked God what it meant, here's what came to mind: there is a version of relevance that is stunning and beautiful, able to take the most complex things and make them relevant to anyone and everyone. Relevant in terms of being closely connected and appropriate to what is being done or considered and to the current time, period, or circumstances (Oxford Language definition). To be relevant is powerful and important. When twisted through the lens of need rather than being, relevance can become a striving to please everyone all the time. This would be my Achilles heel: people-pleasing. A vain impossibility that everyone would find me pleasing and a waste of time that my actions often arise from it. It's the skewed version of the God-given desire I have for relevance.

How do I know this? Conversations with God.

Let's Review

Anyone can hear God regardless of what you think you think about God. Everyone has access. It's a secret hidden in plain sight but few know it: all can hear, all the time, period. You may not know it yet. You may not have experienced it yet. You may have questions, lots of good questions. The reality is still the same regardless of your questions or experience: everyone can hear God now.

I would say that I'd go to my grave defending this but I never really need to defend this because it's so true that in people's experience of it, no more proof is needed. Arguments to the contrary generally cease in the space of reality.

How? In your thoughts. You are already hearing (or thinking with) the voice of God sometimes, not all the time—you just didn't know it. Just because you can hear Him anytime, doesn't mean you are thinking with God all the time. There is much choice involved here.

Think of it like a conversation with someone. You have much to choose: how often to engage, how long to engage, what to ask or not ask, how much you actually want to receive and process what they say to you, whether you stay checked in and engaged or simply act like you are. You may choose not to speak but to enjoy or not enjoy their presence. All these same things are true about your conversations with God.

Why? Because God is always present. If you had a friend that was always in the room, you may not talk to them much at times, but if they were there, you could. So God's here whether you know it or not; you *can* have a chat. It's that simple. For those inclined to theological arguments, the simple concept of God being Immanuel is enough. If God's with us, really with us, and it's more than conceptual, you can talk to God. God is always speaking (oftentimes without words) to us in every language.

This works out well for those of us who would like to have a chat. Turns out, you can.

Here's the quick and practical how-to, but if you want more, I'm dedicating an appendix to this at the end of the book.

How to hear God now:

1. Have a mental conversation.

2. Record all your thoughts for real.

3. *Sort,* don't judge.

4. Repeat as often as desired.

Have a mental conversation: if you need to write it out like a play with speaker names and then the thoughts that come to mind, great. Do that. So it might look like this:

Cayce: (now I'm going to record exactly what comes to my mind as I think, but at some point, I'm going to engage in a conversation like God's really in the room, even if I'm skeptical) I don't know what to write. I don't know what to say. I'm not sure how to do this. This just feels like a stupid nothing journal entry. What am I doing? Oh yeah, recording my train of thought and starting a conversation. I feel tired. Why am I thinking about a gray cloud of smoke?

I need to get to the store soon, also need to make a list for dinners this week. Shoot, I'm distracted. Oh yeah,okay, God, are you there?

Now as soon as you "pass" the conversation off, meaning you pause to listen to someone other than you or you ask a direct question to God, now you will need to record again exactly what comes to mind right after you think the question or give pause for another voice.

God *(note that the thoughts will come in the same way and sound the same as your own voice. Record them anyway!)*: Yes, I am. Right here. Whether you know it or not. This seems like I'm making it up. Of course God would say "here!" I already know that about God.

(You could keep on going especially if you are willing to ask more questions and record the answers.)

Record all your thoughts for real: even if you don't write out every single thing like a play, do record the conversation in some way. Jot down notes on paper or in your notes app.

Sort, **don't judge:** now let's go back and check it. Usually the "God words" come fast and immediately after you pass the conversation that way. Like we ask kids who come for prayer at ONE, "Who's faster, you or God?" "GOD!" they say and they have no problem hearing God immediately after they ask a question turned in God's direction.

Look back at what you wrote and find what feels authentically like your voice and your questions in the conversation. Look back at what came immediately after you asked God something or paused to listen. Notice if any of the thoughts that came are critical or abusive. Those you can sort into the "other" category. Your sorting will look like this.

Three categories: God, you, other.

How do you know which is which? The Hearing God chart helps. The chart helps you understand the difference between what comes from love and what comes from fear. If it's God, it will always sound loving. Have you ever heard something that's hard to hear from a place of love? It actually feels good. God's voice will be kinder than your own voice toward yourself. God's voice will come from a place of freedom and non-anxiety. God's not worried. You might feel anxious. The "other" voice of fear might be whispering to you, but I will guarantee you that any thoughts that come from a place of anxiety are not God, because you came from God who is perfect peace. So any anxious or fearful thoughts can go into the "I feel," so the "you" category or into the "other" category if they simply sound like something anxiety would say.

Recording all your thoughts won't always be necessary, but for now, it is so that you can sort through them and find out what thoughts might be God, what thoughts are your own voice in the conversation, and what is something else altogether.

For some of you, judging is actually judicial and not condemnation-laden. So in that case, you are free to "judge" as long as it's more of a weighing and sorting that is free from any form of self-derision or condemnation. Practical condemnation or judgment usually takes this form in the case of listening for God's voice: "I can't do this, I don't hear God, I'm gonna mess this up, I'm not getting anything, it's not working, this is stupid, I'm just making all this up." You'll have thoughts like that, and it's fine. Just don't let them lead you to stop short without sorting. Sort, don't judge.

Repeat as often as desired: you can insert a God conversation into your day as often as you like. Truly, your ability to hear God's voice anytime is completely unlimited in reality. It has only been limited by your thoughts about it in the past because if you think you can't, that will be your experience.

There is more you can and will do as you grow in practicing conversing with God, but these are the most basic steps. It's as easy as *talk, listen, sort*. Or *listen, respond,* and *check*. Checking matters: if I think God just told me to go kill someone, I clearly need to take the time to "sort" that thought. Does it sound like love? No. Okay—not God, toss that thought out. Or lean into the conversation. That might look something like this (sorry I know, this is extreme, but you get why I need to do this):

> Cayce: God I had this thought come to mind that I need to go kill someone. I'm not sure where that came from. Jesus, what are you really saying?
>
> Jesus: I love you. That's not my voice or yours. Let it pass.
>
> Cayce: Then what do I do?
>
> Jesus: Take care of yourself and call someone who can help you. I'm here and I'll never leave you.

Another sample conversation that's fitting for this book:

> Ask, "Jesus, I feel _____. What's really going on? What's the threat?
>
> Notice what comes up immediately after you ask. If it's a picture or a memory or an idea, ask an obvious and honest follow-up question next like this:
>
> "Jesus, why did you bring up that picture or what does _____ mean?"
>
> Record what comes to mind next.
>
> Finally ask, "Jesus, real and true?"

Notice what comes to your thoughts immediately after the question.

Go back and check what you think God might have been saying. Look at it and see if it comes from love and produces love (check the root and fruit). Does it come from a life-giving kind place and does it produce life-giving kindness? If not, let it go or use it as a springboard into more self-awareness and more conversations with God.

FINAL THOUGHTS

It took me three years to finish this book. It started as one thing and morphed into another. I wasn't planning to focus on the vibrant parts of being a human that threaten in such deep and mysterious ways. I hear that often a book writes itself through a willing vessel. I don't know about that, but I do know that once I found the flow of writing about those threats, the trajectory of this book would not be detoured. No matter when I sat down to write or what I determined to write about, that is what came out. Of course, if I'm writing to anyone, it's to myself. And I hope it's helpful for you too.

I find that most good things in life can be summed up pretty well by an Avett Brothers song. The lyrics to "No Hard Feelings" have been rolling through my head as I finish up my edits on this book. It dawns on me that we know what hard feelings are but do people talk about soft feelings? Is that a thing?

It could be a helpful way to look at feelings because when we aren't willing to feel our feelings, they get hard. Stuck. Tough. But when we dare to feel them, to look at them and be honest about them, to move through them like kneading dough, to have real and honest conversations about them, then they begin their journey from tough to touchable. Hard feelings have left me feeling untender and disconnected while the soft ones help me see myself in others and vice versa. We really are so deeply connected, aren't we?

As you have thoughts, some may seem so very hard-wired into your brain that they are experienced as old mind ruts, and some of them literally *are* just that, nothing more. Practicing *Mind Alchemy* is a way to take what seems hard or old and soften it. It's a way to knead something that at first may seem tough and knotted, to let it rise, and then to expose it to warmth so it can go ahead and rise just as things with yeast do. Then maybe the furnace of life turns up the heat and what happens in that hot furnace is transformation - fresh bread. Trust that the yeast is in there and as you let life knead you, the deeper, most connected parts of who you are will rise to the surface and will become nourishment to you.

In the first chapter, I referenced a quote by Dr. Daniel Siegel, a neuropsychiatrist about what the mind is scientifically. He calls one facet of the mind "the emergent self-organizing embodied and relational process that regulates the flow of energy and information." That sentence says so much about how and why the practices in this book work. Emergent. Embodied. Relational. The process regulates the flow of energy and information, but what he says next explains why it's so natural for us to live in a state of connected dialogue in our minds. We assume that we are alone up there, even though our "monologuing" is happening with so many different experiences, voices, and ideas. Listen to what Dr. Siegel says next to explain how the mind works (bold emphasis mine):

> The system that we're talking about is a complex system, that means it's open to influences from outside of itself, it's capable of being chaotic and it's non-linear meaning small inputs have large and difficult-to-predict results. When you have those three characteristics, math says that it is a complex system. And once we're in the realm of complex systems we find that these complex systems have what are called emergent properties. The interaction of the elements of the system give rise to these properties that cannot be

reduced to the singular elements that are interacting to give rise to them. The notion that complex systems have emergent properties is sometimes responded to by various scientists or even the general public as very confusing or even ridiculous. What I do in the book *Mind* is I actually put some quotes from scientists who see emergence as not only a scientific property of complex systems, but as a necessary way of understanding what it is that emerges. For example, why clouds have the beautiful ways that they unfold across the sky—that's an emergent property of water molecules and air molecules that form the clouds and the emergent property there is self-organization that is determining how it unfolds.

…So here's the amazing thing, it's a proven property of our universe that complex systems have this recursive property to it. It's probably why people have not really gone to these emergent properties because, especially self-organization, it's not intuitive. The second reason I think people haven't gone here is because this definition of the mind as the emergent self-organizing embodied and relational process that regulates the flow of energy and information **is placing the mind in two places at once, 'within your body' and between you and other people and you and the planet. So this irritates people because first of all, many people point to their head when they talk about their mind and they place the mind inside the skull. But even if you kept the mind only inside the skin-encased body, you'd feel okay with the word embodied and many people do. However, once you say it's both embodied and relational, you get into this really interesting new way of thinking because you say how could one thing, mind, be both within and between—in two places? Here's a way to think about it: the fundamental element we're proposing is energy and information flow. Now if you think about that, neither the**

skull nor the skin are impermeable boundaries for energy and information to flow. So you may think of them as two places but it's one system, energy and information flow, and it's happening in many different locations."

This is why the skill of intentional mental dialogue (technically accessing the mind that's in two places at once) allows you to hear God's voice and at the very least, to actually accomplish far more in your mind, than you imagined you could. Energy and information flow through the mind but are not stuck or contained there. The organs in your body mediate an interconnectedness between us that is literally, not just figuratively, vast and as far-reaching as your ability to mentally imagine. This may not be intuitive as far as our cultural understanding goes and it may go against much of what we've learned in the past that is highly individualistic and limiting, but it *is* actually intuitive. You've been dreaming and processing information that extends far beyond the confines of your mind from the beginning. Without language, you intuitively knew you were connected to a much greater whole beyond yourself as a young child. So much of the adult journey is apprehending what we already knew but did not yet have language or developed practices for. I hope this book helps you make some of these "mind-blowing" concepts accessible and experienceable for you.

I wish you a journey through life where your mind enables you to go with no hard feelings, but many soft ones. With no enemies, and that journey starts within—that your own mind, body, and soul are fully embraced and experienced as a friend not foe.

I'll close with these beautiful lyrics written by Robert William Crawford, Scott Yancey Avett and Timothy Seth Avett.

No Hard Feelings

When my body won't hold me anymore
And it finally lets me free
Will I be ready?
When my feet won't walk another mile
And my lips give their last kiss goodbye
Will my hands be steady when I lay down my fears, my hopes, and my doubts?
The rings on my fingers, and the keys to my house
With no hard feelings
When the sun hangs low in the west
And the light in my chest won't be kept held at bay any longer
When the jealousy fades away
And it's ash and dust for cash and lust
And it's just hallelujah
And love in thought, love in the words
Love in the songs they sing in the church
And no hard feelings
Lord knows, they haven't done much good for anyone
Kept me afraid and cold
With so much to have and hold
Mmm, hmm
When my body won't hold me anymore
And it finally lets me free
Where will I go?
Will the trade winds take me south through Georgia grain?
Or tropical rain?
Or snow from the heavens?
Will I join with the ocean blue?
Or run into a Savior true?
And shake hands laughing

And walk through the night, straight to the light
Holding the love I've known in my life
And no hard feelings
Lord knows, they haven't done much good for anyone
Kept me afraid and cold
With so much to have and hold
Under the curving sky
I'm finally learning why
It matters for me and you
To say it and mean it too
For life and its loveliness
And all of its ugliness
Good as it's been to me
I have no enemies
I have no enemies
I have no enemies
I have no enemies

Songwriters: Robert William Crawford / Scott Yancey Avett / Timothy Seth Avett

APPENDIX A—
TODAY'S BOX,
TOMORROW'S WISDOM

After you've completed a helpful Out of the Box session on your own, here's a three-week guide for integrating that wisdom into your daily life.

Every day for the next three weeks, we'll refer back to your recent "Out of the Box." After that, you can repeat the three weeks or move on to another "Out of the Box" process.

Each day will take no more than ninety seconds to complete. Here's what I suggest: pick a time before 9:00 a.m. and put this book in front of you so that you have to run into it first thing in the morning. At your feet when you wake? By your sink? By the coffee machine? In your front car seat? Whatever works for you to do ninety seconds in the first portion of the day.

At the end of the day, before you go to bed, you'll simply look at the bottom section of the page for that day. Repeat each day for twenty-one days—easy!

DAY 1

Take thirty seconds to scan your completed "Out of the Box."

Circle the top three phrases that stand out to you. Don't overthink it; you only have a few seconds. Go with what jumps out on your first scan. What's highlighted in your mind?

Write them here:

_____

_____

_____

Now circle one of them. Put a star by the one you are most drawn to for today.

Close your eyes and imagine (or ask Jesus to give you a picture) what it looks like for this freedom to be integrated into your life today.

Write down the gist of what you got with your eyes closed so you remember later:

_____

_____

_____

_____

_____

Have a great day! Check back in tonight here:

Before Bed:

Write down what stands out to you from today, good or bad, interesting or uninteresting. Take twenty seconds to write what is most forefront on your brain right now. Brain dump:

_____

_____

_____

_____

Scan the page above and notice the way that what you did for ninety seconds this morning impacted your thoughts and actions today. This is a gratitude space. Find something you can honor or be grateful for about the way this practice impacted the day:

_____

_____

_____

_____

Go back to your "Out of the Box." Notice what one thing stands out to you now at first glance. Write it here and we'll start here in the morning.

_____

_____

_____

_____

_____

DAY 2

Rewrite the last thing you wrote that was highlighted at the end of yesterday:

_____

_____

_____

_____

Go look at your "Together We Can" statements and pick one thing that you will take action on today:

_____

_____

_____

_____

Take what was highlighted to you that you wrote first and think about it in light of what you will move into action on today. Think specifically about the motivation for your action. Where does the action come from? Desire, insight, wisdom, hope? Great! If you feel any residual "should" in it, take twenty seconds to look beyond it for the deeper motivation for your actions. If there is none or if it's less than joy or if it isn't desire driven, then table it. If it's from desire and joy (P.S. "Joy" to the brain is this: someone's glad to be with me, not exuberance. That "someone" can be you, another person, or your experience of God. It's a non-anxious belonging type of presence). Go for it.

If tabled, why?

_____

_____

_____

If moving into action, what does that look like, and by when in the day?

_____

_____

_____

_____

See you tonight!

Before Bed:

Take hope: Think of hope as the umbilical cord that connects us to the womb of God. That's what the Hebrew words for "Hope in God's mercy" mean. What do you have to hope in right now? What connects you to that Source of unending nourishment, growth, protection, and provision? Look at areas that you can actually have agency or choice in. You're looking at where there's hope as far as *you* are concerned, not hope that others will change or do something differently (not your territory; you are only responsible for you).

_____

_____

_____

_____

_____

_____

Give yourself permission on a deep level for that hope to integrate and impact all of you—especially as you sleep. Let it wrap around and settle into you.

DAY 3

If you dreamed about anything last night put it here:

_____

_____

_____

_____

_____

_____

_____

_____

_____

While this isn't a dream interpretation book, remember these key things about dreams:

1. They are almost always helping you process and are almost never literal.

2. People and places usually represent parts of yourself or your circumstances. Don't assume that your dream is about the literal people you dreamed about. Usually, people represent the qualities you first think of when you think of them, but it's often actually about you.

3. Symbolism is at its finest in our dreams, so don't freak out when you have weird ones!

Go back to your "Out of the Box." This time we're gonna take a deeper look just at the flowing river. Read it out loud over yourself twice—that's two whole times.

Have a beautiful day!

Before Bed:

One more time, read the flowing river part of the "Out of the Box" out loud over yourself or have a friend or your partner read it over you.

Go to sleep and rest in deep peace.

DAY 4

Get out *all* the thoughts in your mind. No sentence structure is needed: Go! No editing!

Go back to your flowing river and highlight your favorite statement that's there. Put it here:

_____

_____

Have a lovely day. See you tonight!

Before Bed:

Look at your "Shoulds" and "Oughts" (Top and left inside of box). Take a minute to find the top three that just aren't relevant to you now or that never were very sticky for you in the first place:

_____

_____

_____

Now that you've put them there, see if they have any hook or pull in you. If they don't, just mark a line through them. If they do hold a bit of sway with you, no problem. It's just a chance to get more out of the box. Take ten seconds to write one more "Out of the Box" statement. Ask God, "What do you want me to know from your heart to mine?"

_____

_____

Sleep in peace!

DAY 5

Time to check out your vows, must-nevers, and always have-to's on the right side of the box. Look them over, and then revisit the top of the page where you landed outside of the box.

Highlight two things you notice as you reread the top:

1. _____

2. _____

Based on the above two highlighted statements, notice just one way that you could change something small about your normal routine to create a new and different outcome for yourself or others.

What will you do differently today?

_____

_____

_____

By When: _____

See you tonight!

Before Bed:

What happened today with your small change today?

_____

_____

_____

_____

How are you feeling as you end the day? Use one or two words or sentences to describe these three areas for you currently:

Heart: _____

Mind: _____

Body: _____

Ask God the same questions now, about you:

"God, you know me better than I know myself. How would you describe how my heart feels?"

_____

"God, you know me better than I know myself. Wow would you describe how my mind feels?"

_____

"God, you know me better than I know myself. How would you describe how my body feels?"

_____

Notice the similarities and differences between your perspective and God's. What's interesting to you?

_____

_____

_____

Rest well, friends.

DAY 6

Take five deep breaths, the kind that fill your belly first, front and back, then your middle, front and back, then the top of your chest last, front and back. Let them go fully and slightly loudly. Let it out.

Take one more breath in and take as long as you can to breathe it out while you read the bottom portion of your "Out of the Box" page—the foundational action. As you read it, keep breathing for at least four counts in and six counts out.

One more time, read the bottom section: "Together, we can…" *while* breathing in four counts and out six counts.

Have a great day!

Before Bed:

Breathe deeply, fill the deepest part of your stomach front and back, then fill your middle, and last, your chest front and back. Let it out hard and fast. Do that again three more times.

Now change to four counts, breathing in deeply, and take at least six counts to release all the air. Notice if there's any stress you are holding in your body that you can release while breathing out.

Notice what one thing stood out to you today from your practice this morning. Write it here:

_____

_____

Give yourself permission to dream about it both in your sleep and in your waking moments as you drift to sleep.

Good night!

DAY 7

You may or may not remember your dreams from last night. If you dreamed last night, write it down here:

_____

_____

_____

_____

_____

Remember, "bad dreams" aren't actually bad.. They represent and indicate all kinds of things that can be helpful. Pay attention to the emotions in the dreams and the symbols. You might find something present in your dream that you are ready to release or get curious about today. You also might find something present in your dreams that is encouraging, life-giving, or thought-provoking; embrace it and find one good question to ask God about it.

_____

_____

_____

What are you dreaming about in your waking hours?

If nothing, give yourself permission to dream about life and what "could be" for sixty seconds:

_____

_____

_____

_____

Keep dreaming today. See you tonight!

Before Bed:

Go back and read what you wrote above. Add any detail or further thinking here:

_____

_____

Now reread the very top and bottom portions of your "Out of the Box" tool. They start with "Your Name" at the top and "Together we can" at the bottom.

May your dreams be filled with the beautiful collaboration of daytime dreaming and nighttime processing. Your mind was designed to filter and further brilliant thinking at night. Value this incredible design feature that you have as a human.

Good night!

DAY 8

In ninety seconds we are going to do an "Out of the Box *quickie*"—short and sweet:

1. Draw a box right here. Divide the box into quarters.

Ask what "shoulds" you are holding today: put them in the first quadrant.

Ask what "oughts" you are holding today: put them in the second quadrant.

Ask what "musts" or "nevers" you are holding today: put them in the third quadrant.

Ask what "would if I coulds" you are holding today: put them in the fourth quadrant.

Now ask about each statement in the quadrants and put the deeper, wiser answer outside the box somewhere.

Great. Have a fabulous day!

Before Bed:

Revisit your mini "Out of the Box" from this morning and let it fill your mind as you prepare to lie your head down.

Take five full, deep breaths as you read it to yourself two more times, and then let it go and go to bed!

DAY 9

Start with a brain dump for forty-five seconds:

_____

_____

_____

_____

_____

_____

_____

_____

_____

Great, now take ten seconds to express something you are genuinely thankful for:

_____

_____

_____

_____

_____

Now that you have shared, listen to God and pen what comes to mind: "God, what's on your mind?"

_____

_____

_____

_____

What do you notice that encourages you?

1. _____

2. _____

3. _____

Go on with it! Have a lovely day.

Before Bed:

Reflect on the three encouragements that you experienced this morning.

What happened throughout the day?

_____

_____

_____

_____

What do you want for your tomorrow?

_____

_____

_____

_____

Sleep tight!

DAY 10

Look at the bottom of one of your boxes. What would you do if you could?

Now take it further out of the box...Together We Can, either express yourself more fully or ask Jesus for more from His heart to yours:

_____

_____

_____

_____

Before Bed:

We're gonna do the exact same thing tonight that we did this morning. See if you get the same answers (feel affirmed in that), or if there's more (be grateful for the more):

_____

_____

_____

Give your heart, mind, and body permission to play with these ideas as you sleep and when you wake!

Before Bed:

Take twenty seconds before bed to speak these things out loud to yourself in whatever words make the most sense to you.

Good night!

DAY 11

This is a rest day. Pause: breathe, celebrate yourself for sticking with this for eleven to twelve days and *go* back. Look at Days 1–10 and notice what stands out to you that you can acknowledge. Scan it pretty quickly and write below what stands out to you:

_____

_____

_____

_____

_____

_____

_____

Have a fabulous day and find a way to honor yourself and your processing thus far!

Before Bed:

List five people that you look up to, even just for one particular thing about them:

1. _____

2. _____

3. _____

4. _____

5. _____

Go to bed with gratitude for their enhancement of your own life at the forefront of your thoughts.

Good night!

DAY 12

Do a self check-in:

My heart feels:

_____

My mind feels:

_____

My body feels:

_____

Now ask Jesus: "Jesus, how does my heart feel?"

_____

"Jesus how does my mind feel?"

_____

"Jesus how does my body feel?"

_____

What do you notice?

_____

Great! Have a fabulous day!

Before Bed:

Tonight, I honor the risk I took today in this area:

_____

Tonight, even if things didn't go as I expected, I value this insight:

_____

Tonight, I choose to look and see how connected I am to other humans and the world:

_____

Tonight, I take a minute to look at the power and impact of my choices. I see it in these ways:

_____

As I go to bed, I lie down and release these judgments:

Of others: _____

Of life: _____

Of myself: _____

Sleep tight!

DAY 13

Take a minute to look at the flowing areas of your Out of the Box. Pick the ones that feel full of the most ease and grace for you.

Put them into this sentence: Today, I choose to step into the gracious flow of:

_____

Take five deep breaths, into the depth of your stomach front and back, then into your middle front and back, and now into the top of your chest front and back, release.

Now take five deep and slow breaths of at least four counts in and six counts out.

Before Bed:

How did you experience flow and ease today?

_____

What did grace look like for you today?

_____

DAY 14

Write one area you want to see more joy in personally:

_____

Write one area you want to see more creativity in career-wise:

_____

Write one area you want to see more freedom in interpersonally:

_____

Go back to the top of your first Out of the Box and read it out loud. Now revisit the three statements above and write one thing by each one that you can do, however small, to BE or *embody* joy, creativity, and freedom there.

Have a lovely day!

Before Bed:

Write a vision statement for what it means for your life to be what you want it to be. What do you really, really want?

This isn't just a superficial question about things you might want, though you may have to start there to get deeper. Go beyond that to the core of what you actually want to look back on in your life and say you experienced. What you will have been glad that you spent your hours and energy on.

At the end of the day, what do you really, really want?

Take ninety seconds to jot some things down. Tomorrow we'll keep going, so for tonight, just start thinking and noticing what comes up.

_____

_____

_____

_____

_____

_____

_____

_____

_____

DAY 15

Set your timer for ninety seconds and answer as much as you can get through. Go!

Joy—where do you experience the MOST joy? List what comes to your head first:

_____

Hope—what do you hope to get out of life? When it all is said and done, what would you like to say that you did?

_____

Contributed to?

_____

Experienced?

_____

Enjoy this gift of a day. See it for what it is (an abundance of opportunity) and don't let anything make it what it's not (lacking).

Before Bed:

*Go back and pick up where you left off above. If you made it through it all, go back and refine it.

May your nighttime dreams move you further toward your waking dreams.

DAY 16

What keeps you from hoping? I don't mean hope as cross your fingers and "hope" things go right. I mean what do you genuinely and actively hope for in your own life and the lives of those you love?

_____

_____

This is another way to say, "What do you want?" Hope also says, "This is what I want and believe can happen one way or another." Go back to your Out of the Box and look for places where you see hope deferred, held back or squashed. What do you notice?

_____

_____

_____

It's said that hope deferred makes the heart sick, but a desire fulfilled is a tree of life.

Notice what pokes at your hope. What sparks it? What deflates it? If you note that it can be poked or swayed easily, pay attention to that and ask why?

Is there an area of life where you feel heart sick?

_____

Ask God, "How have I experienced hope deferred?"

_____

Now ask, "What desires have You given me that can act as a tree of life to me?"

_____

Before Bed:

What did you notice about the way "hope" goes for you throughout the day?

_____

What actions do you see yourself taking that are motivated by hope or clearly not connected to any hope? How does hope exist for you, practically speaking?

_____

What creates the feeling of life and free flow for you? How can you practice that and integrate it into your day tomorrow?

_____

DAY 17

Where has hope been deferred in your life—the overarching story of your whole life?

Take ninety seconds to think back and forward—what seeds of hope that existed in your life are there that just never blossomed?

_____

_____

_____

_____

_____

Now go back and highlight one that matters to you, even if it seems very far-fetched or unrealistic. Give yourself permission to highlight the one that has a spark for you. Leave shame in the corner or kick it out the door. This isn't something you have to share with anyone, so pick the thing that really is deep in you that has felt squelched or unnoticed. *Circle it.

Before Bed:

Go back and re-circle what you circled this morning and take a few minutes to let the dust fall off of it. What about *that* particular thing sparks life, fun, and desire for you?

_____

_____

_____

_____

What if this could act as a tree of life to you? What would it look like to accept and embrace this deeply seeded desire? Can you imagine what you look like with that desire in full bloom in your life? Write what that would look like. Ask Jesus, "What do I look like when I have embraced that hope/desire?"

_____

_____

_____

_____

Great, now sleep on it.

DAY 18

Please take one second to draw a tree (it won't be good, who could do that in one second?).

Please take ten seconds to draw a tree (you'll be impressed how much you can do with nine more seconds. :)

Please take twenty-five seconds to draw a tree. This time make some obvious branches on both sides that you can go back and write on. Don't worry, there's no wrong way to do this except not to do it at all. No-judgment art zone here.

Great work. That's it for now.

See you tonight!

Before Bed:

Go back to your one-second tree art. Take either your hope from Day 17 or one of the things that you really really want to get out of this life from Days 15–16 and put it on the trunk of that tree.

Now go to your ten-second tree drawing. Again, write the desires for your life on the trunk, and then put the parts of your life it affects, influences, or adds value/meaning to in the tree canopy. If you don't have a canopy on your tree, use your words to make it.

Last, go to your twenty-five second tree drawing. Use the branches as places to write out what your life would look like if that particular dream/desire/passion was to take root and produce a harvest in your life. What would your life look like if that thing flourished and developed?

Sweet dreams! May your deep desires unfold in your sleep whether you are aware of it or not.

DAY 19

Time to revisit your first Out of the Box. Start from the very inside, the middle of your box: the situation/box/issue that you were breaking out of. Notice what has changed about the issue/situation or yourself in the past three weeks.

_____

_____

Now look at a very key piece of Out of the Box that we haven't honed in on yet: the underlying "fear of _____" beneath the right inner side of the box (the vows/will-nevers/must-always side).

Take thirty seconds to think about the way that particular fear has influenced your life:

_____

Ask God, "What would my life look like if that particular fear was gone?"

_____

Now ask, "How has this fear helped me cope in one way or another?"

_____

We don't make friends with fear for no reason. It is feeding us something. Maybe it's making me feel safe to feel afraid? Sounds like an oxymoron but it's a very real thing for many of us. For example, we think that if we are afraid of being unsafe, we'll be safe. Subconsciously we mistake fear for responsibility. This is an illusion that legitimizes the perpetuation of fear in my life even if it's not actually protecting me anymore.

Take a look at times in your life when this fear worked on overdrive. Ask God: "What outcome was fear driving me toward or away from?"

_____

Ask, "What did fear produce in my life or keep me from producing?"

_____

Usually this will land somewhere in the territory of helping you feel a certain way or not feel a certain way based on circumstances. See if you can find the pattern there.

What were you trying to avoid or attain?

_____

_____

_____

_____

Notice what you notice about the subtle or not-so-subtle voice of fear in your life today.

Before Bed:

Look back at what you wrote this morning. Where are you now?

_____

What do you notice about how that particular fear seems to affect you on the day-to-day?

_____

Ask God to bring to mind a time in your life when you felt totally at peace. Trust what jumps into your mind first, and go with it even if what comes to mind first is unexpected.

Let's explore that memory for a few seconds. How old are you? What does it feel like? Smell like? Indoors or outdoors? Is anyone else in the memory? Go ahead and let your thoughts wander around and notice what's there in the memory. Give yourself permission to "belong" there again.

_____

_____

_____

In your own words, express gratitude for what you just remembered:

_____

Now ask God: "Why was that memory brought up for me today?"

_____

Good night!

DAY 20

Today, we'll jump right back in where we left off last night. Same song, second verse. Trust what comes to mind this time. It may be the same space or it may be a different one. If a new one pops into your mind even subtly, take a peek into it and really go there, like you did last night.

Ready?

First: go to a place in your memory that is a place of peace, love, or safety. Take a few minutes to really explore what pops into your thoughts. What does it look like? Feel like? Smell like? Notice what you notice.

Go ahead and "belong" there again.

Take a second to express honest gratitude for what you are remembering. What are you grateful for about that memory?

_____

_____

From that memory, see what happens when you bring the fear from your Out of the Box into this space of belonging? Notice what you notice about what happens to it.

Notice what happens to that fear when you picture it being exposed to light. Notice God's kind of separation taking place around that fear. Notice ground and seeds and grasses and trees rising around that fear. Notice what happens when you picture that fear in the backdrop of the stars at midnight. Notice what abundance says to that fear. Ask God what it looks like to move past that fear and dismantle it. Now what happens when you rest? When you breathe deeply and release yourself from the fear as if it's an old husk falling away from the seed that is your life?

Here's an example from my processing: There was a time as a kid when it seemed I was afraid of everything. I could easily work my way into an overwhelming, trembling fear if I let myself go down a fear trail. Then there came a point where I learned to flip a switch and the thing that once made me tremble, I could now both talk about and laugh at. Fear became very disempowered when I could laugh at it instead of tremble at it. So when I personally just went to a past "safe place," what came to mind was my home as a child of ten. I remember times I felt terrified as well as times when all the fear melted because I was able to see that it was actually nonsense. A made-up story in my mind, a nothing. It actually became very funny. So from this place in my memory that came up today of being able to remember laughing at fear, now I will process the fear that came up in my Out of the Box process which is "the fear of being wrong."

Trust what comes to mind when you think of a safe memory space. If you do this again tomorrow, something different may come up and that's normal. Fear always tells us false stories about who we are and what we really want. To live from that story will trick us into behaving in ways that are actually opposite of who we want to show up as in the world. Healthy fear keeps us safe, but embodied fear lies to us and tries to keep us safe from a false threat: our true selves.

See you tonight!

Before Bed:

Ask Jesus to bring to mind a space where you felt unconditionally loved and safe. Trust what comes to mind and simply be present for what comes. Rest in it for a minute. Be grateful for it. Listen and look at what Jesus highlights to you about why He brought you to this particular memory.

Ask, "Jesus, what do you want me to know about where You are in this memory?" Notice where you sense God's presence.

From that place of safety, ask Jesus for a picture of some sort of container to use.

Fill that container with anything that feels heavy like fear or shame or anything burdensome. Let it all out into that container: people associated, feelings associated, and anything at all that feels heavy.

Picture yourself taking a step back from it in your mind. Then hand it to Jesus and watch what He's gonna do with it.

Take a few notes from what you just processed:

_____

_____

_____

_____

_____

_____

Ask God, "What do you have for me to feel instead of these fears and these heavy burdens?"

_____

_____

_____

Go back and look squarely at your Out of the Box page. As you look at it, see it not as individual words or phrases but as a big picture—almost as if you're looking from above and can't read what it says, but you can see the whole thing as a picture.

Before you go to bed, I just have one question for you from the macro perspective of your Out of the Box: what do you notice about that fear?

_____

_____

That is an important thing to note.

Now, sleep.

DAY 21

Look again at your Out of the Box. Indeed, fear has been boxed in! This is an important thing to notice about the Out of the Box process. By doing it, you immediately put FEAR *in* the box and yourself *out* of the box. This is a powerful movement.

As Rosalind would say if we were all together in person, "More of *that!*"

You are invited to join us in person for a One Journey Experience anytime. Plan for a seven-day experience broken into two parts. The first three days we dive deep into moving in the creative flow of your life—connected to the authentic you, connected to God, and in healthy relationships with other people. For the second part, a four-day retreat, we dig into your unique core drivers (you have a core question, core desire, and core flow that have been driving your life in beautiful ways and in less-than-beautiful ways). At some point in the seven days, we'll coach you through an Out of the Box, so if you are an in-person kind of person, that's an option you might enjoy. We'd love to meet you.

What else would you like to draw a box around today? Maybe it isn't anything necessarily bad but something you want to understand and look at more closely. Maybe it feels nebulous or confusing. Pick that one.

First, draw a picture that represents this and what's coming to mind:

Now, draw a box around it.

Next, write your full name outside of that box. It can be big, it can go in a circle, it can fill the page—as long as it's outside the box and bigger than the box.

Great! See you tonight—our last night of the three weeks!

Before Bed:

Look back at the box you drew this morning. Who defines who? Does the box define you or have you defined the box? If you'd like to add more detail, go ahead and put the story the situation is telling you into the box. Then take your time listening to a deeper, broader story and put that one outside the box.

If you are able to discern boxes and limits that keep you restricted, see them, articulate them, and move beyond them. What does that mean about you? Ask God.

_____

_____

_____

If we all experience fear about being wrong and small, bad, unworthy, unloved, unseen, unknown, misunderstood, and unimportant…If it's normal to feel shame and want to hide and be concerned that we are a fraud…If we are capable of experiencing, sharing, and expressing common fears that keep us boxed in, what else could we share?

_____

_____

_____

It's fascinating to think about where rivers come from. Most come from a powerful Source somewhere—a rock. Snowfall on a mountain. Heavy rain clouds. Source just is. Connection and expression of Source also is. It's in the realm of what is because what's really true just is. What's not passes away.

You were never actually in a box. Your ability to choose to function within a certain set of rules, paradigms, or judgments shows that you are _also_ fully able to function outside of it with a whole other set of capabilities and resources.

If you were able to live boxed in, it's proof you can live too in the flow.

As you look at the river flow of your Out of the Box, what do you notice and appreciate about the reality of your way of being as described in the flowing sections?

_____

_____

_____

_____

You navigated the world from your boxes and limitations because they were your inverted and hidden intentions. The most powerful way you will move is outside of those limitations in the full, uncovered expression of your God-given desires and intentions.

This isn't a case of bad vs. good. Both are powerful. If you can see that living in the box is powerful because of the energy you bring to it, and it has no actual power on its own, you will be encouraged about the kind of energy you carry innately.

The box requires the power of your will, choices, and strengths; no more is required of you when you move from _outside_ the box. Quite the opposite, out of the box, your effort, energy, and presence will flow with much more ease like jumping in a tube and floating downstream. This honest ownership of your intentions allows for the unique flow of power that arises from inner alignment and integrity (oneness). Another way to describe this is joy-derived energy. It's the "clean burning" heart, mind, and body energy that will grow, teach, and direct our path.

Challenges will still arise. Highs and lows will happen. Breakdowns will occur, but navigating those things from inside the box will ensure you feel limited and caged in as you navigate. Navigating from outside the box ensures an adventure, which you also might like.

Before Bed:

Ask this question of yourself, then God:

"What moves me into healthy action in my life?"

_____

"God, what moves me into healthy action in my life?"

_____

"What brings me into rest?"

_____

"God, what brings me into rest?"

_____

Sleep in peace, giving every part of you permission to rest well, reminding yourself that the One who keeps you will not sleep, so you can relax and surrender to the rest that will heal, restore, and energize you.

Great job on your twenty-one days!

APPENDIX B— RESOURCES, ACKNOWLEDGMENTS, AND FRIENDS

It's hard to discern how much of what I have to offer is really the deep influence of others along the way (99 percent?) and how much of it is independent thought as if there was such a thing. I'm deeply appreciative that my journey would cross paths with these specific people in some way. I'm 100 percent sure their voices and their influences are the reason this book exists.

Nancy Holcomb introduced me to my first experience of inner healing prayer in 2003 and she gave me the book *God Guides* by Mary Geegh. That book taught me to connect with God in a ridiculously simple way and the inner healing prayer showed me what it actually looked like in real life. These are the two resources I didn't know how to ask for when I was twenty, but Nancy showed up with them and they have marked my life trajectory in a strong way. You can find them here… https://god-guides.com/product/god-guides/

Thank you to Dr. Karl Lehman who I have only met once but who has been influencing me from afar for the past twenty years through his writing. Thank you to John and Leeba Curlin who hosted us in their home years ago and taught me that I could have real conversations with God. Healing began flowing in my life the day I came to your home and the river only widened over the years.

Our team at ONE is truly my most valued and respected resources outside of my own family. To know them is to love them. To work with them is a delight to me in every way. You each create a space that is life-giving. I miss it and you anytime I am away for long. I know I have the best job in the world and don't take it for granted that it's because of you. Thank you for loving me and championing my authentic self-expression, cheering me on in my pursuit of showing up honest and free in the world, specifically, in our shared world.

Thank you to Sonia Roper, Rosalind Hervey, Zach Leal, John Walt, Sabrina Thurman, Debora Daniels, Gabrielle Leonard, Jay Heck, and others who created one of my favorite resources and the first published book that I got to be a part of, the *ONE Journal: 49 Days of Hearing God*. I don't know of another book like it. It's simple, beautiful and many say it's been very helpful. It has helped me as well. Thank you, John's team at StacDek. Pair the hard copy with the videos from the drip email course and you have a lovely journey to take at your own pace with a few close friends, family, workout group, team—any group you like—or on your own.

There's one teacher who was most formative in my learning because he taught me how to learn. At sixteen he led me over as many hills in Israel as he possibly could to let my feet begin to understand the land, the culture, and context (pictures, imagery, history) of the stories of God and "God's people." He taught me so much, but there are two things that radically changed everything about the trajectory of my life. I'll outline them briefly below because they are very much a part of this book even if I didn't state it outright:

I had spent my entire life learning the Bible in school but I had no idea what "**The *Kingdom* of God**" was, even though it's *the most prominent* thing Jesus demonstrates, talks about, and teaches. The understanding that the *kingdom* of God is *at hand and within* is foundational for an understanding of practice-able, living dialogue with God. It's the foundation for all good theology and it's another "what is" that I grow in discovery of more all the time.

The *kingdom* of God is not in some far-off future after death, but maybe that too. The *kingdom* of God is not about political dominance and conquest, unless if your idea of conquest is turned on its head and loving your enemies "wins" the day. The *kingdom* of God is not about perfect religious words or deeds (orthopraxy or orthodoxy). Helpful words and deeds usually follow real interaction with the person of Jesus. Jesus mentions something about this: if we've talked with Him and encountered Him, the *kingdom* has come to our house today. If at any point you dove into a conversation with God throughout the book and it brought clarity or peace or perspective and most of all, love to you, you experienced what Jesus called the *kingdom* right there where you are—that's worth the little time that it takes, right? It's engaging! Keep talking, ask good and honest questions, share the conversation with trusted people, and you'll find you are going somewhere special (and that it's not just to Heaven one day).

The other thing I learned from Ray is this: **experiencing context** is everything if we really want to understand the story and engage in the ongoing dialogue of our communities. For us in Israel, that meant walking the land and digging deep into the contextual roots of the Hebrew Scriptures. It changes the way we learn and think. It's humbling because it becomes clear that much of what we thought was "true" was really good-hearted assumptions created without connection to context. Things aren't always what we think they are, and we have to be willing to "unlearn" and not know so that we can grow and learn more. What a valuable life skill: to not be threatened by being wrong in order to develop a deeper understanding. Remember, we are threatened often by a fear of being wrong, but the real threat is that we might grow and develop! Would that be so bad? To say: hey, I got that really wrong before but

I'm open to growing! Ray taught me how valuable that skill is both directly and indirectly.

At that point in my life, I was so hungry for a "heart" experience of God and not just what some call a "head-knowledge" (I liked to shame myself for being heady, just because I liked to study—I was going for that religious master's in self-condemnation). RVL integrated the heart-and-head teaching experience so beautifully. Heart, mind, and body all get to show up and that's when life and learning really get fun and move through our lives (so beautifully declared in the Shema, an ancient prayer from Moses's day likely prayed by Jesus).

Fifteen years after learning for a season from RVL, I met Rosalind Hervey who taught me this: "Here's how humans grow—*Experience before label.*" Think about it; it's by design. As a baby, you experienced a whole new world but had no labels or language for it; that would come later. This just *is* the way we actually grow in health. Ray and Rosalind helped me understand that the kind of "teaching" I wanted to do was practical, experiential, and then, in good time, plenty of space for great conversation together. Growth has everything to do with experiencing things together and then talking about them. Pain, confusion, and insincerity happen when we force labels without experience. Furthermore, when we try to force a corporate or community experience that requires people to serve organizations rather than creating space for organizational structures to serve the community, that same pain, confusion and insecurity is multiplied and religious experiences become oppressive rather than freeing. Rosalind Hervey has shown me with her life what a healing community can look like and just how vital it is to helping us grow. Healing community is the experience that the western church is so desperate for but we haven't had it modeled well for us - it's the opposite of oppressive religious structures competing to be right about the "truth."

This is why we create spaces for people to actually practice the connection they already have with God together. *Together, it always goes better.* That's not just a nice phrase—I see it every day in our work. We need more people practicing and sharing these things with one another in a safe, nonjudgmental way because we have so many words about God and they are easy to find almost anywhere. In my experience, few are practicing *words with God,* together in a way that engages everyone. RVL and Rosalind, you have modeled and taught this beautifully. I appreciate you both so much.

The Last Word on Power by Tracy Goss came at just the right time in my life. Someone, thank you from the bottom of my heart whoever you may be, sponsored me to participate in Tracy's Executive Reinvention Program a few years ago which was the answer to many of my life questions and prayers. I learned so much from the experience and the friendship. Thank you to Tracy and her coaching team. You can find Tracy's book here…

https://www.amazon.com/Last-Word-Power-Tracy-Goss/dp/0795348053

So many dear friends that I am grateful for but conversations with these three in particular water my soul in such a rich way that writing became easy. I have learned so much from and with the three of you: Anne Marie Bailey, Kelley Feste, and Kim Wolfe.

To my community of friends, I am a wealthy woman because of you. You know who you are, and you're each intertwined in the pages of this book even if not named outright. You teach me and you love me well. *Thank you for seeing me and for letting me see and know you.*

My family—you are my heroes and my true joy in life! To my kids - Jaden, Hudson, Claire, Yates, and Lee - each of you are the greatest gifts I will ever know! Everything I write is ultimately for you, my loves. My parents, Lil and Mike Yates are the definition of hitting the familial jackpot. To Joel, we have grown into so much of this together and I will forever thank God for you in my life.

Have questions or stories from your experience reading *Mind Alchemy*? Ask them directly to me through video and I'll reply! Curate is an app you can find in Google Play or the Apple app store - it's for you and your community to connect through video pods. Download our Curate app and use this code to find the Mind Alchemy pod:

Code: Mind-67718

Cayce is the Director of ONE, an oil and acrylic artist, and she hosts The One Journey: a guided, interactive seven-day experience for small groups of leaders. The One Journey is a unique mixture of a retreat, workshop, and coaching with great meals and accommodations on the Texas Gulf Coast. Cayce and the ONE team will help you discover your core drivers and experience personal Out of the Box practices. More info available at www. theonejourney.com

AFTERWARD

A personal update and my wish for you

Breakdown leads to breakthrough is one of my favorite phrases. It has brought comfort in the middle of the hardest seasons. It's a promise that life won't always be this way. It's not an empty promise but a truth to discover experientially throughout your one, beautiful life.

There *is* light that will dawn after that dark.
There *will* be resurrection on the third day.
There *won't* always only be darkness, your soul is pure light.
When I placed the final paragraph in this book, I was thrilled to be finished. Then, I was completely shocked by what began almost immediately to unfold for me: the breaking down of my marriage.

It wasn't a sudden betrayal or a new element that surprised us and sent us reeling. It was a reckoning of our lives. It was almost as if the words I wrote in this book demanded that I engage them on a whole other level than I had previously in my life.

In the rest and the surrender, after the writing, the words on these pages asked one thing of me: was I willing to engage them more deeply and truly in *every* area of my life?

Was I willing to push past certain fears that had held me hostage my entire life?

Was I willing to be brave and honest enough with myself so that I could face the mountain right in front of me that I had been ignoring, evading, trying to tunnel through and hike around for so long?

Would I take the next step forward toward the kind of personal integrity and alignment that only I would know about if I did not?

The threats got loud. Looming largest: if you actually show up fully honest, you will hurt all the people you love most in the world.

For me, this was vow territory: **do not** *hurt people.* To hurt people I love is not just undesirable, it's a personal threat tantamount to death for a very simple and profound reason that I found out months later in therapy: I could not hurt people (especially those I loved most) because I was very hurt by people.

No amount of me avoiding hard truths in the name of avoiding pain (*causing* pain) actually protected the people I loved. The threatened state of unreality that I was stuck in for years was this: ignore your pain to protect your people.

The past 6 months have been a crash course in learning to move past what threatens me most in order to reclaim the parts of myself that I had abandoned for very good reasons.

I abandoned my inner child long ago in order to protect her. I kept practicing habits that seemed logical but were really self-destructive to make myself feel good about controlling life for my nearest and dearest.

At some point, all our best attempts to protect, hide and control even for great reasons, will fail.

This book is for those seasons. If you find yourself in a season you couldn't have imagined till it arrived, you are not alone. You are seen. You are known. You are loved.

This book is to remind me and to remind you that you won't die when you move past what threatens you. You will find life beyond the breakdown, even the ones you cannot now fathom.

It's September 2023, since March, when I finished the book, I have separated from my husband and we have filed for divorce. This was never, and I mean not *ever,* what I imagined my life would look like. This was not part of the plan. It is a fabulous goal to be the couple who makes it to the 50th wedding anniversary and who the kid's friends point to as the real deal. Fabulous goals can cover over the greatest of threats and let me tell you, I was so threatened to fail at *this*, of all things - not this.

What threatens you isn't inherently about whether it's good to be threatened by it or not (ex: it's good to not want to hurt people or get a divorce) but the nature of threats is that they bully you into hiding, self-deception and they require you to think lesser thoughts of something (yourself, your future, your family, the world) in order to remain in charge. If you are being personally kept by a threat or trying to keep something together because you are threatened by its loss so deeply, you will live a less than integrated life, possibly for the remainder of it.

My greatest wish for you and for me is that you learn to easily recognise when the threats are keeping you safe rather than the life-giving words of God. Showing up honest with God, yourself and your most trusted friends will keep you in a place of healing - healing is a process and at times, it will feel like a threat. Be strong! Trust the path ahead even when you don't know if you can trust anything else. You are not alone!

The words you receive from God are words that will kindle the fire of your life that cannot actually be quenched. They are rooted so deeply in your very own heart, soul and mind that they will always catalyze life-giving breakthroughs, take courage! The life within you, as you let it rise up and surface - becoming conscious of it and face to face with it - is the reason that the saying is true: breakdown leads to breakthrough, always.

If you find your world shaking and quaking, suddenly hit by a personal earthquake and all your threats rise up to meet you - take a deep breath and let the life in you rise up too.

As you are threatened, remind yourself that it's not only going to be ok, it's going to be better than ok - it will be beautiful.

The paradox of life is that somehow your greatest breakdowns will break through to true beauty every single time. Look for it, wait for it, imagine and envision it.

Love and life will find you there in the most difficult of places and take you to the home you didn't know you were made for - *your own* beauty.

I speak not from theory but from the very present reality of my life.

Finally, a prayer. May you know this through experience:

Yours is light. *Yours* is God's kind of separation. *You* are grounded. The stars dance over your head and the sun *will* keep rising. Abundance *is* your birth-right. You move, even on the hardest days of your life, *with* God. Rest. Be loved. You have your very breath, your movement and your full being in the God who literally dwells within you.
Feel it.
Relax in it.

Savor it.

Get present to it again and again.

And when you feel the old threat of fear lurking near, **be** not afraid my friends. Because the truth is that even to see it for what it is means you are so very brave.

You, amazingly made human, will always **be bravery** embodied in flesh and bone. You could never be fear embodied. it's not in you or of you.

May you know, deep in your soul, that all threats will ultimately work for you, reminding you who you really are and how far you've come. You and fear were never one.

You are one with the Creator of **all** - *all* wisdom, *all* joy, *all* hope, *all* truth and *all* life.

Sit, walk, stand and sleep in the reality of ***all that*** wherever you might find your feet today.

With Love and Joy,
Cayce

I mentioned Tracy Goss multiple times in the book and she wrote an endorsement for the book a few months ago. At the time of publishing, September 2023, Tracy died. I wrote a tribute to her and I'd like to share it to honor and remember her life. What a gift to have known her and to have loved her.

I'm so sad to hear the news of the death of this legend.

She had me sing the song "More" by Madonna in my first Executive Reinvention Program, with a few Tracy edits of course.

How could I know then how much the song would come to mean to me not just that year, but specifically this year?

Tracy Goss, you were so much more.

You were more than a coach to countless people like me - more than a coach, a thought partner. More than a thought partner, a transformation master, more than a transformation master, a reinvention genius.

More than a genius, you taught us how to be a human. More than cracking open our humanity, you did it as our friend. More than being a real friend, you were a mother.

A mother not in a sappy sense of the word, but the kind of mother we needed: you embodied a wisdom that challenged us, a chutzpah that invited us into a whole new way of being and a candor that pierced necessary holes in our egos.

More than being a mother, you were MORE present - taking a stand on the power within us - than anyone I've ever met in my life.

Some might say (you wouldn't) you were more of a spiritual mentor than any they'd met before.

More than being a radically empowering force in our lives, you quite literally created the kinds of clearings where anything and everything could happen. And it did.

I don't think I could write more and mean it more about anyone else.

You had an absurd impact on the world. I am deeply sad you are gone. I only wish I'd taken the chance to tell you a few more times how much I love and respect you.

At the same time, I know that it was enough, as were you. It was you who taught me, in the midst of making me sing about "More" that I was completely and fully enough. Enough and free…

More free than ever, rest in peace Tracy.

Thank you for living your one life in such a beautiful way - you were right, we only get one of them and I can hear your voice echo in my mind after reminding us that you knew a man who died by a boulder falling on his car on the highway, "What are you going to do with your ONE extraordinary life before you die?"